FIFE COUNCIL LIBRARIES

HJ281053

Please r~ ~ before

Amanda Holden

the biography

Amanda Holden

the biography

jim maloney

JOHN BLAKE

FIFE COUNCIL LIBRARIES	
HJ281053	
ASKEWS & HOLT	15-Feb-2012
920HOL	£16.99
BIOG	AY

www.johnblakepublishing.co.uk

www.facebook.com/Johnblakepub   facebook

twitter.com/johnblakepub   twitter

First published in hardback in 2011

ISBN: 9781843583561

All rights reserved. No part of this publication may be reproduced, stored in a
retrieval system, or in any form or by any means, without the prior permission in
writing of the publisher, nor be otherwise circulated in any form of binding or
cover other than that in which it is published and without a similar condition
including this condition being imposed on the subsequent publisher.

British Library Cataloguing-in-Publication Data:

A catalogue record for this book is available from the British Library.

Design by www.envydesign.co.uk

Printed in Great Britain by Printed in Great Britain by CPI Mackays,
Chatham, ME5 8TD

1 3 5 7 9 10 8 6 4 2

© Text copyright Jim Maloney, 2011

Papers used by John Blake Publishing are natural, recyclable products made from
wood grown in sustainable forests. The manufacturing processes conform to the
environmental regulations of the country of origin.

CONTENTS

INTRODUCTION

'My motto is, "Never give up."'
AMANDA HOLDEN

The face is radiant under the glare of the studio lights as the TV camera zooms in close. Wide eyed with her mouth opening in wonder, she looks up at the stage, almost mesmerised by the performers.

It could be a child enraptured by watching her first pantomime, or a teenager in awe of her favourite pop star. But this study of enthralment is one of the biggest celebrities in the country and fast becoming a star in America.

After a long and successful acting career starring in some of the top dramas and comedies on British television, Amanda Holden is at the pinnacle of her professional life. As one of the judges on the hugely popular Saturday-night prime-time series *Britain's Got Talent*, she has the performers, along with a TV audience of millions, hanging on her every word. While her former co-judges, Simon Cowell and Piers Morgan, were often cutting and brusque in their comments, Amanda has always been kinder and more encouraging. And that's because she knows what it is like to perform on stage, and the determination and nerve required to achieve your dream. Be it dancing dogs, burlesque strippers or escapologists, Amanda has time for them all because she admires their spirit.

Over the years Amanda has taken many knocks, both privately and professionally. Her parents split up when she was four and later in her life she faced the wrath of the public's hostility when she had an affair with actor Neil Morrissey while married to Les Dennis. She has also suffered the heartache of two miscarriages within a year. Along the way she has had to endure some crushing criticisms of flop comedies, such as *Celeb*, *Mad About Alice* and *Big Top*. But after each blow she has bounced back stronger and shown incredible resilience.

Her work ethic is second to none. Always striving for more, she has moved from one job to another and, as well as the flops, she has starred in some of the most successful shows on British television: *Cutting It*, *Wild at Heart*, *The Grimleys*.

Amanda has shown she can take the knocks in life. She only ever wanted to be a famous actress and set about reaching that goal with a relentless enthusiasm.

'I don't take no for an answer and pursue everything I

want to do until I've exhausted every possibility,' she has said. She had rehearsed her Oscar-winning speech at nine years old!

Having tackled comedy and drama, in 2003 she took to the stage to realise a dream role as the star of the West End musical *Thoroughly Modern Millie*, surprising many with her singing and dancing prowess.

Following her disastrous marriage to Les Dennis, Amanda met the record-company producer Chris Hughes, whom she described as her 'soulmate'. They have a daughter, Alexa (or 'Lexi'), who was born in 2006, and the pair married in 2008. Today she is happy and settled with her family but she retains that drive she has had since she was a young girl to keep striving for more. And, when Simon Cowell asked her to be a judge on *Britain's Got Talent* in 2007, she eagerly accepted. It was to send her stardom soaring.

The show became a TV phenomenon and Amanda found she loved every minute of it. To her surprise, she enjoyed it more than acting and has said she would happily continue being a judge into her 90s.

However, she is frequently reduced to tears on *BGT* by someone with a hard-luck story to tell or a singer with an unexpectedly beautiful voice. Her teasing co-judges have ribbed her about it and there have been some suggestions in the press that she is overacting, but she says the emotions are real. She has had to develop a hard shell to get where she is but inside she has always been soft. She adored her grandparents and being a mother has made her even more emotional so, when an elderly or young singer walks out on the stage, Amanda already feels a lump in her throat. And she says she is touched by parents who go on the show in an effort to make a better life for their families. She's also an animal lover, so that pretty much covers all of the acts!

But Amanda's ambition stretched wider than this country and she always craved success in America. She flew out frequently to be introduced to people who might help her career but each time it came to nothing. Her big break Stateside came just when she thought it would never happen. To her surprise it was *BGT* that did it, or – more precisely – a certain singer nicknamed SuBo.

When awkward-looking Susan Boyle walked out on the stage in 2009, nobody expected what was to follow. Already there were a few sniggers in the audience and, when she remarked to Simon Cowell that her voice was a bit like Elaine Paige's, he – now notoriously – rolled his eyeballs. But within a few moments everyone in the studio and those watching from home were transfixed by the beautiful sound that came out of her mouth.

Boyle launched into 'I Dreamed a Dream' from the musical *Les Misérables*, a song that mesmerised a nation. It was such a golden TV moment that it was put on the YouTube website and SuBo also became a sensation in the US. They couldn't get enough of this unlikely-looking singing sensation and invited her onto numerous chat shows. And the clamour for SuBo led to Amanda and

Piers Morgan also being invited across the Atlantic to talk about her. Amanda saw her chance and grabbed it!

Amanda's sparkling appearances on American television, talking about all things SuBo- and *BGT*-related, led to more regular appearances until she landed the job of UK entertainment reporter on the CBS TV morning news programme *The Early Show*.

'For years I went over to America trying to make it. But I'll be the first to say that I owe it to Susan,' she said.

The year ahead is a challenging and exciting one for Amanda Holden and she is going to be as busy as ever, dividing her time between stage and TV, between Britain and America, as she juggles a transatlantic career with marriage and motherhood.

As well as *BGT* – with new co-judges David Hasselhoff and comedian Michael McIntyre – she was thrilled to be asked to cover the wedding of Prince William and Kate Middleton on 29 April 2011 for CBS. And she has taken on another West End musical in May, playing Princess Fiona in the stage version of the hit cartoon movie, *Shrek*.

She has always been outspoken, and her honesty and wicked sense of humour have got her into trouble in the past. She can sometimes give the impression of being over-exuberant but she is such an honest character she probably can't help herself when she blurts out a jokey comment that she is likely to regret. But, despite the knocks and flak, Amanda's adage is that the show must always go on.

'I've got my mum to thank for an absolutely brilliant and blissful childhood, which is why I think I've got so much confidence,' she has said in interview. 'My mum says I probably came out singing. At one time, I would write twenty letters a day to producers, and phone contacts and my agent every day to check what they were doing. There have been plenty of tears along the way and, at times, I haven't always had my priorities right. But I've never, ever considered giving up. I've always been a bit of a performer and a show-off.'

ONE

STARS IN HER EYES

'She's going to be a star, that girl.'
<small>ANGIE BLACKSTOCK ON AMANDA HOLDEN</small>

As a young girl Amanda Holden dreamed of fame and bright lights, and was determined to make it as an actress. But such a life was a world away from where she grew up – in the quaint and picturesque country town of Bishop's Waltham. Nestled in the rolling hills of the Meon Valley in Hampshire and situated between Winchester and Portsmouth, the historic town is a mix of ancient buildings, thriving shops and businesses, and a handful of fine inns.

Steeped in history, Waltham is believed to date back to ad 500, when Saxons settled there. It gained its prefix when Bishop Henri de Blois, brother of King Stephen, founded Waltham Palace and St Stephen's church in 1136.

Today, the peal of eight bells from the beautiful St Stephen's Church still rings out every Sunday, deafening the nearby Georgian houses and echoing beyond, as if boldly to remind everyone that this ancient place of worship is still very much a part of the community.

'I adored growing up in Bishop's Waltham and have fond memories of being taken as a small child to feed the ducks on the pond at Bishop's Waltham Palace, and of picnics in the grounds with my grandmother, parents and little sister,' Amanda was later to recall.

But her early childhood was marked by a traumatic event that would shape her future life and help form her into the strong, affectionate, fun-loving personality we all recognise today.

Amanda's parents split when she was just four years old. Frank and Judith had met on a blind date in Gloucester and married on 6 June 1970. They bought a house together in Bishop's Waltham. But their relationship sailed on stormy waters almost from the beginning.

Frank's job as a petty officer in the Merchant Navy had taken him from his native Liverpool all around the world and his lengthy time at sea was hard for Judith – particularly after the arrival of their first child, Amanda, on 16 February 1971. A year later, their second child, Debbie, was born and Frank's long absences from home now meant double the trouble as far as Judith was concerned. Bringing up two young children on her own, with little money, was difficult. She took on an assortment of part-time jobs to help make ends meet, working as a secretary, barmaid and fruit picker.

Amanda's earliest memory is helping her mum wash Debbie in a yellow plastic bowl. 'She was newborn and crying her head off. I was only sixteen months old. I was probably trying to drown her but Mum thought I was being helpful – the dutiful older sister!'

'Our marriage became increasingly fraught,' Frank recalled years later. He would come back with exotic tales from the Far East while she had been alone with the two small children. Yet Frank insisted he cherished the moments when he was there with his family. 'Amanda was a very good baby, very quiet, sitting in her pram, observing the world. I was very happy. I was married, with our own house and two cute little children I adored.'

Frank says he played a game they called 'horsey-horsey', allowing them to ride on his back. He bought them an upright piano, which he painted white and gold. He also recalls taking them for walks in their double buggy. 'There are no words to describe the feeling of hearing your little girl say, "Daddy."'

But the marriage was fast steering towards the rocks and was about to capsize. 'I was based at HMS *Collingwood* in Fareham, Hants, when Judith asked me to leave the home because she was fed up of the absences.' Amanda was four and Debbie two. Frank returned briefly a few months later as they tried to mend their marriage but it proved to be irreparable and he departed for good. Shortly after the split he was drafted to Plymouth. 'I had two hours' access a week on a Sunday, no transport and very little money, so I reluctantly made the decision not to visit but to keep in touch at Christmas and birthdays,' he later said in interview. 'I thought turning up for just a few hours a week would disrupt their lives – not mine – so I made what I thought was the best decision. With hindsight, it was the worst decision of my life and I bitterly regret it.'

Frank sent Christmas and birthday cards, and presents, but it would be many years before Amanda saw him again. 'I just feel very sorry for my real dad because he lost out on two fantastic children,' she recalled.

Frank's own childhood had been a traumatic one in which he suffered from a broken family. His mother died aged 38 from a blood clot when he was just 18 months old. His father, a well-known Liverpool banjo player, also called Frank, was unable to care for his six children alone, so Frank junior and his twin sister were sent to an orphanage and later brought up by guardians. Frank senior, who became a psychiatric nurse, killed himself in 1983.

'Like me, Amanda grew up not knowing her father. It's very sad the way that part of our history has repeated itself.'

But by the age of five Amanda was already calling another man 'Daddy'. Judith had struck up a relationship with a local man, Les Collister, who became the girls' much-loved stepfather. Les was a popular figure who played for the local football team and worked for a garage owner, refurbishing old cars. The two girls took a great shine to him and were delighted when he married their mother when Amanda was 12.

'Mum remarried a wonderful person who has been the man I think of as "Dad" since I was five,' she said.

Life at home with Judith and Les gave the girls the love and stability that they needed. And Amanda would later talk about the many fond memories of her childhood. 'Dad was the greatest in the world. He's done all the things dads do and brought us up as his own. My parents worked full-time, so I suppose we were latchkey kids. During the week we'd get home from school, and me and my sister would watch *Grange Hill*, always making sure the telly was off and the table was laid by the time my mum got back.'

Amanda remembers that, if ever she was ill, she would sit with the quilt and watch children's TV shows such as *Bod* – 'which I loved' – or *Jamie and the Magic Torch*, and her mother would make her egg sandwiches.

'We never had pudding. My mum always said, "If you're still hungry, have some bread and jam."'

The girls had a very close relationship with their mother but, by all accounts, Judith didn't make the mistake of spoiling them and Amanda later related how she got a short sharp shock when, at the age of five, she let her yearning for a sweet get the better of her.

'I stole a fruit salad, one of those chewy little sweets, from a shop. I was incredibly pleased with myself and thought Mum would be too. So I showed her the sweet and, to my surprise, she went mad. She dragged me back to the shop by my ears and I had to hand it over. I got a real telling off and Mum said I was never to steal anything else again. And I haven't!'

Amanda eagerly looked forward to the annual Bishop's Waltham carnival, which still takes place each June today. The main road is closed to traffic as children and adults, dressed in colourful outfits befitting that year's theme, take part in the parade. Amanda loved dressing up and, as she walked along the road, lined either side with spectators, she already felt like a star.

A favourite family holiday was to go camping in Cornwall.

'We used to camp around Polperro. I loved it. Even now, if I hear a zip being done up, it reminds me of my mum tucking me into my sleeping bag at night. I have memories of buckets and spades, and eating sand sandwiches and cockles in polystyrene cups on the beach.'

While Debbie was the pretty, girly one, Amanda was the extrovert who liked to show off and was forever putting on shows for her family – whether they liked it or not!

'I was singing from the age of three. I'd make up dance routines and perform *Annie* and *Grease* in the back garden. I'd get the kids in the street to take part. And we'd charge people five pence each to watch.'

And the drive and ambition that were to serve her so well later in life were evident even then. She gave up ballet lessons because, as she explained to her parents, she had her own shows to direct! She would often 'treat' her family to shows she wrote and performed, often wearing a pink blanket emblazoned with the words 'Dancing Queen'.

'I used to rush down on a Sunday, turn the telly off – even if they were watching it – and make up song-and-dance routines,' she said.

But, if Mum and Dad sometimes felt a little jaded, besotted Granddad Jimmy was often there to proudly tape Amanda and Debbie's performances.

Amanda has always been one to push herself though and already she had her eyes on TV. She wrote to *Jim'll Fix It*, the popular BBC TV show in which DJ Jimmy Savile helped make kids' dreams come true. Amanda asked him if he could 'fix it' for her to dance with Legs & Co., the dancers on *Top of the Pops*.

'When I didn't hear a thing back, I was gutted.'

Amanda started going to church-hall dances when she was six. Her dance partner was a local boy named Clifford Culver and they began 'dating' when she was ten.

'Clifford was my first boyfriend. He used to come round for tea, although I've no recollection of kissing him. We went ice skating and he'd pick me up when I fell over. Mum and Dad used to tease me about him. He and I wore braces on our teeth at the same time. It was all very innocent. He was a sweet boy.'

A proud moment for Amanda was when she won a local dance competition. Her prize was the 12-inch version of 'Young Guns' by Wham! 'It was thrilling because I'd beaten all the other kids in the village.'

Mum and Dad had to endure watching a variety of dance routines from their precocious child after they bought Amanda her first record for her eighth birthday – 'I'm in the Mood for Dancing' by the Nolans.

Although she was a keen gymnast for a while and trained several nights a week, she soon set her mind on becoming an actress. Never one to set her sights low, at the age of nine she practised her Oscar acceptance speech in front of an amused Judith and Les!

'I thought it was quite moving. I'd thank everyone involved in the film, my parents and then my husband, without whose love and support I could never have done the job. But, if I ever get up there, I expect I'll fall apart and only thank my mum.'

Ever starstruck, Amanda also rehearsed for when she would be interviewed as a famous actress. Her favourite magazine, *Look-In*, had a regular back-page interview with a celebrity, and Amanda would read it and then give her own answers to the questions. Yet she insists that her quest for fame was perfectly natural. 'I've always wanted to be a famous actress. Anyone who says they want to be respected for the profession they're in and they don't want to be famous is lying.'

But Amanda wasn't the only performer in the family. Bishop's Waltham had a thriving local drama group, the Little Theatre, and Les, Judith, Amanda and Debbie all enjoyed going there.

'They called us the Von Trapp family!' Amanda recalled.

But, while for her family it was a fun and sociable activity, Amanda was far more serious. It was here that she learned the rudiments of what was to become her profession and, even at a young age, she stood out.

The Little Theatre was run by a woman named Angie Blackstock, who remembers the moment when she knew that Amanda had the star quality and drive to succeed.

'We were putting on *Babes in the Wood* and Amanda didn't like the part she was given but, when she heard the applause, her eyes glittered. I said, "She's going to be a star, that girl." Amanda found out everything about the theatre and worked at it like you would not believe.'

It's not difficult to see where the extrovert and fun-loving side of Amanda's character comes from. 'Mum loved anything theatrical. She once arranged a trip to see a stage production of *'Allo 'Allo* in London. She thought it would be really funny if everyone went in fancy dress. She is somewhat flat chested and so decided to wear Kenny Everett-style fake breasts. My dad just went with onions around his neck. They looked totally ridiculous and I said I didn't want to be seen dead with them!'

On another occasion she dressed up as Cher to re-enact her favourite singer Meat Loaf's video of 'Dead Ringer for Love' in the family living room. But exhibitionist Amanda hated her mum having her turn 'centre stage'.

'She wore this purple catsuit with poppers, which she then unpopped to reveal a black bra. She couldn't dance for toffee. I was like a typical Harry Enfield teenager.

I remember saying, "What the hell are you doing? It's not funny."'

Amanda was also down in the mouth when she had to go into hospital to have her tonsils removed when she was nine. It was supposed to be a three-day stay but, when two of the children there contracted foot-and-mouth disease, the ward was sectioned off and she had to remain there for ten days until they were given a clean bill of health. All visitors had to be sterilised and wear a mask, and Amanda couldn't stop crying. The experience may not seem that harrowing to an observer but even today Amanda describes it as one of the worst moments of her life.

'I cried every day for the ten days I was in there. At nine I understood what depression was.'

At 12, she moved to Swanmore Secondary School (now renamed Swanmore College of Technology), a mixed comprehensive in the neighbouring village. Her music teacher, Rosemary Cross, would later say how she noticed her dedication. 'We used to have a music competition in which we encouraged everyone who felt brave enough to offer something,' she recalls. 'When she was about fourteen, Amanda and two friends wrote a pop song and performed it. It really was quite stunning. She was superb. She sang and danced with great skill and confidence. You get a lot of good kids but she had something extra. She gave everything.'

Apparently, Amanda had even invented a stage name for herself – the not entirely glamorous 'Beverley Saunders'. And she persuaded friends to call her by it.

Amanda's exuberance and natural talent led to her becoming a leading light in local pantomimes and musicals.

'Amanda was our gang leader,' says a friend of the time. 'There were about ten of us and she always had us doing exactly what she wanted. She was good fun and never got into any serious trouble. She was one of the goody-goodies.'

One former school pupil recalls, 'She was so confident in the way she did things. Always the centre of attention.'

But such was her willpower and influence that, when there was a teachers' strike – a time when it might be supposed that most children would delight in having a day off – Amanda organised an advance 250-strong pupils' counter-demonstration.

Amanda had been made a prefect despite her extravagantly coloured clothing and eyeliner but she was heartbroken when she was stripped of her prefect's badge in the fifth year after she ate whisky-laden cake for her friend Claire's birthday. 'I was reported, and the deputy headmistress took my prefect badge and sent me home.' But, fortunately, she was reinstated after her mother talked to the school.

Despite her outward confidence and natural vivacity, Amanda never considered herself to be pretty. On the contrary, she thought she was something of an ugly duckling.

'I was never one of the pretty girls at school,' she said in interview. 'When I was twelve I had buck teeth, short hair and a brace. It was supposed to be on for two years but I used to bend it myself, just the front bit, so I managed to get straight teeth in just eleven months. But I didn't feel like the ugly girl at the back of the class either because my parents were always very sweet and complimentary about me and my sister when we were growing up. I've always been a gregarious person and I always fitted in, not because of my looks but by using my personality. I was the kind of girl who talked and joked in class, and I was always popular.'

Amanda had yet to acquire the art of flirtation and seduction. And she learned the hard way that terrorising a poor lad into submission was not the way to win his heart.

'I was dying to go out with a lad called Jonathan Walker,' she would say. 'He was my friend Lucy's brother. Finally he was pinned up against a wall and made to say he'd go out with me. I phoned him an hour later to ask if he wanted to take the dogs for a walk but he said he didn't want to go out with me after all. I was devastated.'

Her first crush as a little girl was on Dave Bartram, the lead singer of the retro Teddy-boy band of the 1970s, Showaddywaddy. The group dressed in traditional drapes and crêpe-soled shoes, and had hits with the likes of 'Pretty Little Angel Eyes', 'Three Steps to Heaven' and 'Under The Moon of Love'. Each time they appeared on *Top of the Pops* she would rush forward and kiss the TV. Judith always knew when Showaddywaddy had been on: there would be lip smears all over the screen. Later Amanda went for pretty boys. 'I moved on to Adam Ant and Boy George,' she said, 'so I must have had a thing about men in make-up.'

Her first kiss was with fellow school pupil Matthew Bishop at a local disco at the Dynamos Football Club in Bishop's Waltham when she was 12. But it almost put her off kissing for life! 'I was going out with Matthew and I went to give him a peck, and he snogged me. I pulled away, disgusted. I told him he kissed like a slug! But I adored him because he looked like Bobby Ewing from *Dallas* and was the school heartthrob.'

When Amanda was 13 her musical taste had changed and she decided to become vegetarian after being influenced by famous veggie Morrissey, lead singer with the Smiths. 'I became a Smiths fan and announced that "meat is murder" [the name of one of their albums], which nearly gave my mum a heart attack. In those days vegetarians were only in hippie communes, not Bishop's Waltham!'

She has remained pretty much vegetarian ever since but it seems those Friday fish-and-chip nights made a lasting impression on her.

'I do still eat fish,' she says. 'So I think I'm really a pescatarian now.'

Money was still tight and Amanda resorted to devious methods to get what she wanted. When she desperately wanted new shoes, she hid one of her old ones behind the wardrobe so that Judith had to buy her a new pair.

'My sister was furious because she knew what I'd done. Mum cleared out my wardrobe one day while I was at school and found it. She went ballistic when I got home because there was nothing wrong with them and they were still a perfect fit.' On another occasion she was forced to wear a winter coat that had belonged to a cousin. 'I hated it so much I got all my friends to tread on it and I dragged it over a bramble bush so that the lining ripped.' Judith gave in and bought her a donkey jacket.

To earn some extra cash Amanda got a Saturday job in the village fruit shop when she was 13. She took home £14 a day and lots of fruit. 'I had a fantastic time with all that exotic fruit, like kumquats and lychees – all the stuff we never had at home. My friend Lucy Matthews used to work with me and, on Saturday afternoons, we'd go to the Moonaz boutique round the corner and spend our wages on clothes.'

Whisky-soaked birthday cake aside, she recalls the time she had her first proper taste of alcohol. In typical fashion, she attacked it with gusto. 'I filled a couple of plastic glasses with red wine and knocked them back out of sight of my parents. I had a terrible hangover at school the next day. I felt dreadful but I didn't learn from it.'

Like millions of teenagers the world over, she was heavily influenced by the biggest female pop singer of the 1980s, Madonna. And she dressed accordingly: puffball skirts, stilettos, lacy fingerless gloves, pearls and pink necklaces. 'I had my hair tied up in ribbons and I remember my first pair of red stilettos, which were my pride and joy. I wore them everywhere with little ankle socks.'

Amanda was about 15 or 16 when she began to pay more attention to how she looked. One of the first things she did was to have a perm. 'Until then I had no concept of how I was perceived physically at all. Not like now. Children are so aware. In my day we never really subscribed to magazines. We just had fun, and it was a bit more rough and tumble.'

When she was 16 the family moved from Southampton to Bournemouth, where they ran a guesthouse, and their family routine changed. All of the family were expected to help out, and Amanda and Debbie would do everything from serving meals to the guests to cleaning the toilets. 'We never sat around the table as a family after that, except for on Sundays. Whatever the guests were having we would take downstairs and eat on our laps in front of *Coronation Street* or *Emmerdale*.'

Amanda's attention seeking and urge to shock were never more evident than when, at the age of 18, she rode around Bournemouth naked on a motorbike. 'I did it for a bet. It was only a pound. I was actually the passenger. We drove past the posh Chase Manhattan bank and waved at the doorman, and he waved back! It was summer – I wouldn't have done it otherwise!'

But her wild side never got in the way of her focused ambition to realise her dreams. She attended the Jellicoe Theatre at Bournemouth and Poole College, where she studied drama and English.

An early indication of her attraction to older men was

when she had a crush on Jellicoe Theatre tutor Charles Lamb, 23 years her senior. 'It started off as a silly thing. Then it turned out real. It was a major crush. He was nothing to look at but he sounded like Sean Connery, and he was so bright and so sexy in his teaching. I wore a very short skirt, a turquoise jacket and a boob tube to show him what he was missing – but I don't think he really realised how much of an impact he made on me.'

Together, her Jellicoe tutors, schoolteacher and Angie Blackstock of Bishop's Waltham Little Theatre helped to instil in her a sense of belief in herself and her future. 'I believed completely that I was going to be an actress.'

Looking back on her childhood, Amanda doesn't dwell on her natural father. The love, laughter and support that followed are her overriding memories. 'I had the best childhood and best parents,' she says. 'I have come from a very stable, loving home. They wanted me to get an education and do my A-levels, and encouraged me to join the local theatre club. I think my mum would love to have been an actress but she was never pushy.

At the age of 17 Amanda left home to join Mountview Academy of Theatre Arts in north London. To supplement her grant she worked in a shoe shop for £30 a day and got a discount on shoes. But the transition wasn't easy. No longer was she the star pupil. Here there were many other fame-hungry students who loved the limelight.

'It was strange being in a room full of people just like

me and trying to get my voice heard,' she later explained in interview. 'I was always a big fish in a small pond. Then, when I got to drama school in London, I met these girls who were loud, made jokes, did impersonations and were just as good or better than me. It was such a shock.'

But Amanda had an idea how to take a shortcut to fame – of sorts. While still at Mountview, she made her first appearance on TV in one of the biggest shows of the period, guaranteeing her an audience of millions.

TWO

AN ACTOR'S LIFE

'I like experienced, mature men.'
<small>AMANDA HOLDEN ON HER PREFERENCE IN MEN</small>

Blind Date was a huge Saturday night favourite in the 1980s and 1990s, reaching an audience of 17 million at its peak. The concept of the show, hosted by Cilla Black, was to introduce three singles of the same sex to the studio audience and, while Cilla asked them a series of questions about themselves, another member of the public sat on the other side of a divider and ultimately had to choose, unseen, the one they wished to go on a blind date with. The screen was pulled back to reveal the person they had a chosen and they would then pick one of three envelopes to see where they would be going on their date. The following week they reported back on how they got along.

Amanda loved the show, and she and her friends would talk about each Saturday's episode the following Monday at theatre school. Animated discussions would break out over which of the contestants was the best looking, who was the funniest and who the date from hell.

There were plenty of extroverts lining up to be on the show who knew that saying something outrageous or wearing a sexy or lairy outfit would get them noticed. As well as 'characters' whose mission would be to make people laugh, it was the perfect platform for a show-off.

Amanda applied to be on the show in 1991 and was ecstatic when she received a reply informing her that she had been successful. She excitedly told everyone she knew that she was going to be on and started planning what she would wear straightaway. She always enjoyed shopping for clothes but now she was on the lookout for something very special – an eye-catching outfit for her big moment on TV. After several failed missions she found just the thing: a black skin-tight, halter-necked catsuit. She made an impact even before the cameras started rolling. She held up filming when amused studio technicians discovered she had nothing on underneath to which they could fix a microphone.

Amanda sat in the middle of two other contestants, hoping to be chosen by the man on the other side of the screen. When Cilla Black, using a peculiar expression, asked which man she would most like to have a 'knees-up' with, Amanda replied that she had four men in mind but, if she had to choose one, it would be Jack Nicholson. Cilla was surprised that she had chosen a man 34 years her senior but Amanda explained, 'I like experienced, mature men.' Although Amanda failed to be chosen for a date, she loved the experience and was even more determined than ever to become famous.

After graduating from Mountview in July 1992, she wrote a cheeky letter to the *Coronation Street* casting director suggesting that it was time the show had a hairdresser and that she would be perfect in the role. 'I thought we should see where Phyllis Pearce [a popular character] got her blue rinse done,' she later joked. 'Of course, after that, the character of hairdresser Fiona Middleton was introduced. I took all the credit, naturally.' The actress who played Fiona, Angela Griffin, was later to become one of Amanda's closest friends.

A year later Amanda landed her first TV role as a murder victim in a drama documentary series called *In Suspicious Circumstances*. Each week Edward Woodward introduced an episode containing two separate dramatised real-life murder mysteries. Viewers were then invited to try to work out 'whodunit'.

The following year, in an ironic echo of the nickname given to her family at the Little Theatre, she was cast as Liesl von Trapp in a touring production of *The Sound of Music*. Amanda, now 21, was enjoying life to the full. Things were on course professionally, her confidence had grown and she was aware that her looks and flirtatious personality attracted men.

She was never particularly 'girly' or subtle in her approach to anything in life and that included dating. On the contrary, she was often more raucous in behaviour and racey of comment than the men. She has always spoken her mind and put her heart before her head, although it has got her into plenty of trouble.

While in *The Sound of Music*, Amanda began dating a fellow cast member named George Asprey. After they split she started a relationship with the orchestra percussionist, 25-year-old John Bannister. He was infatuated with her. 'She was utterly captivating,' he recalls. 'One night, after drinks, we ended up in bed. It was a natural thing to do. It was spontaneous.'

But, while Amanda appeared to think that her relationship with George Asprey was over, the matter was not so clear-cut to George himself. Bannister recalls, 'George found us canoodling in her dressing room. He walked in without knocking, then said to Amanda, "I want a word with you," and she went out. All I heard was, "Yes but I told you. I told you we were finished." She had told me their relationship was over.'

After a few months of dating each other, Amanda took John to meet Judith and Les at their B&B in Bournemouth. She also introduced him to her biological father Frank, with whom she had recently been reunited.

Frank, now living in Devon with his partner Pauline Long and working as an operative on the Torpoint Ferry, had left a note addressed to Amanda at the Theatre Royal,

Plymouth, where *The Sound of Music* was playing, saying that, if she would like to get in touch, he would love to see her.

'Not a day went by without me thinking of the girls,' he later said, 'but I felt I couldn't just snowball back into their lives when they were growing up. I always knew I'd wait till they were adults and let them make their own minds up if they wanted to see me. Amanda appearing in a play nearby seemed like fate was sending me a sign. I just wrote expressing a desire to see her but thinking that, after all that time, she probably wouldn't want to.' Then Amanda contacted him to arrange a meeting.

'When she rang to say yes, I broke down in tears, I was so happy. Amanda was pleasant but to the point. She wanted us to meet at the theatre a few days later.'

Amanda promised to bring Debbie along and also her boyfriend John Banister. But any thoughts that Frank may have harboured of being the errant father returning to the warm embrace of his offspring were soon dashed.

A nervous John arrived early and the wait just added to his anxiety. 'Amanda said, "Let's talk first." And from that moment she called me Frank, not Dad. We crossed the road into a café. The conversation was a little strained as it's hard trying to fit eighteen years' worth of stories into a short meet. I asked them all about their lives and can remember saying I'd seen photographs of Debbie, who was a model, in a magazine. She seemed delighted I'd followed her career.'

Frank later said he was proud that Amanda was performing at the Theatre Royal and told her so. He recalled that the day was an emotional one for all of them, with so much to say and too little time in which to say it.

'I will never forget it,' said Frank. 'Amanda and John seemed very close. I thought I was meeting my son-in-law-to-be. I was quite taken with John. I thought he was a lovely fella. We had a few drinks together and we got along well. We watched *The Sound of Music* show and went backstage afterwards. We were really impressed and proud. I said to Pauline that I could die happy because I'd seen my daughters again.' Christmas cards and the occasional letter were exchanged but it would be another nine years before they saw each other again.

Meanwhile, after they'd been together for six months, John's feelings for Amanda were growing ever stronger. When the tour arrived in Glasgow, he proposed in the middle of the street just before a cast lunch. 'It was completely spur-of-the-moment,' he says. 'We walked up the road a bit, and I got down on one knee and said, "Amanda, will you marry me?" She simply replied, "Yes." I gave her a hug and we went into the restaurant, and I announced it to the rest of the cast.'

But little did he suspect what would happen when the play moved to Bournemouth's Pavilion Theatre. At the first-night party Amanda was introduced to a well-known face who was performing nearby. The meeting was to change her life for ever.

THREE

MEETING AND MARRYING LES

'It was the best day of my life.'

AMANDA HOLDEN ON HER WEDDING

L es Dennis was a household name. At the age of 11 he won a Butlin's talent contest and went on to work the tough Northern club circuit with his mix of jokes and impersonations. His big break came in 1974, when he was 20, on the popular TV talent show *New Faces* (a forerunner of *Britain's Got Talent*). Although he failed to win, he was in good company. 'Victoria Wood was on the show with me and she didn't win either,' he recalled.

Les was born in Liverpool, one of four children. His dad managed a betting shop and his mother was a factory worker at Lucas Aerospace. A shy, retiring boy, he was encouraged by his mum, Winnie, to join the drama group at school and, to his surprise, he discovered he could make people laugh. Playing other characters on stage meant that he did not have to be his real self and this enabled him to come out of his shell.

In her youth Winnie had her own showbiz dreams. She had sung solo in the Liverpool Cathedral choir and had been offered a spot in a talent show when she was 14, but her mother wouldn't let her enter and said she should concentrate on finding work in the factories. Seeing how comfortable her young son looked when he was on stage, she was determined to give him the chances that she had never had.

During a holiday at Butlin's in Pwllheli he was a big hit with holidaymakers, doing impressions on stage. Winnie started chauffeuring him to various gigs across the country, encouraging him to battle his nerves, which dissolved once in front of the curtains.

'A lot of people do impressions to begin with. Mine were something to hide behind,' Les later explained. 'I didn't have to be myself. I was a different person. That was immediately obvious when I started out. My mum could see that I wanted to do it but that I needed that nudge. But she wasn't a "showbusiness mum", she didn't drag me there.'

Les reported that his dad thought it was all a waste of time. 'He couldn't believe that anyone from a working-class background could be an actor or an entertainer. He wanted me to get a "proper job."'

After *New Faces* Les, who had married childhood sweetheart Lynne in 1974, was a regular on TV light-entertainment shows. He was one of the team on the anarchic comedy series *Russ Abbot's Madhouse* and *The Russ Abbot Show*, and went on to forge a successful double act with fellow young comic Dustin Gee, and they were given their own TV series, *The Laughter Show*. The pair were enormously popular, appealing to all age groups with their clean-cut, family-oriented act. Les was at his happiest. Having a partner to work with, and to talk to on and off stage, eased his nerves. But, tragically, the good times ended suddenly. Dustin died of a heart attack in 1986, leaving Les devastated.

'It's a lot easier to be on stage with somebody else because you can have a laugh and work off each other. Being a solo comic is the loneliest business in the world,' he said. 'If you've had a bad time and go back to your digs, it can get soul destroying. Really, you're only as good as your last show and every time you go on stage you feel you're auditioning.'

Les felt that the best way to cope with his pain and loneliness was to throw himself into his work but he was later to realise that he had made a mistake in not giving himself enough time to deal properly with his grief. 'Looking back, I think the most difficult thing was going back into panto the day after Dustin died. At the time I was told all those clichés like "the show must go on" but I wouldn't do it again. I was worried about other people instead of thinking of having time out for myself. I just carried on and bottled it all up, which didn't come out until a year or so later.'

Feeling lost and lonely without his good pal and partner, Les took over from Bob Monkhouse as host of the popular TV quiz show *Family Fortunes* in 1987. It proved to be just the vehicle he needed, offering stability and a high profile away from the strain of stand-up comedy. He remained as host for 15 years until 2002.

But Les believes that his grief and depression contributed to the break-up of his 16-year marriage to Lynne, with whom he had a son, Philip, in 1980. 'Instead of grieving, I ploughed myself into work,' he says. 'I must have bottled up so much. I just carried on and my marriage was the casualty. It was a terrible time.' Les left his home and family behind in Liverpool when he moved to London. Between 1977 and 1986 he was hit by a succession of traumatic events – both his parents died, so too had Dustin and then his marriage broke down. Now he had to learn to adapt to living on his own without the support of family and close friends in bustling London.

An emotional man, Les was still coming to terms with the loss of his partner when he turned up at the Bournemouth Pavilion Theatre in 1993 for an opening-night party. Bubbly, fun-loving Amanda Holden was in an even more effervescent mood than usual, still enjoying the buzz of having just come off stage in *The Sound of Music* at the Pavilion Theatre.

Les, then 39, was appearing at the end of the pier in the farce *Don't Dress for Dinner* with Lionel Blair and *Hi-de-Hi!* star Su Pollard. He was also a well-known face to Amanda, as host of one her favourite childhood TV shows, *Family Fortunes*.

'We had a first-night party for the Pavilion and invited the Pier Theatre along,' remembers Tony Hardman, publicity officer for both theatres. 'That was when they met.'

'I thought he was a miserable sod and he thought I was loud!' Amanda later said was her first impression. 'My friend Emma was talking to him, and I came over and told this very rude story about how my nipples play up in cold weather. Les just stared at the floor with his hands in his pockets.'

'She was bright and bubbly,' Les would later reveal. 'Apparently, I was a right miserable sod. I was distracted at the time. My son Philip was fourteen. Me and his mum had split, so it was his turn to stay with me. He and a mate were at my rented flat, and I was itching to get away from this party to see they were all right. I was aware of Amanda – you couldn't be anything other – but we didn't connect.'

But there appears to have been at least some interest on his part because he later told the *Sunday Mirror*, 'At the time I felt my life was over and that I was destined to be alone for ever. I hated myself and believed I didn't deserve to be happy. It sounds corny but I literally spied Amanda across a crowded room.' Amanda was starstruck but was dealing with it by acting overly confident. She admitted to being instantly attracted to him. 'I fancied Les from the moment I saw him. I've always been attracted to older men. Jack Nicholson is my ideal but Les is just as sexy. He had gorgeous blue-green eyes and I like blondes but it was his manners that mattered most. He was gentlemanly. He's also got lovely chunky legs.'

Over the summer they would bump into each other in Bournemouth and they struck up a friendship. Les later described how their relationship blossomed. 'We kept meeting at functions and I found myself going to more of these events than I normally would. But it was three weeks before it dawned on me that I went because I really liked being around her. We started seeing one another properly and I realised this was something serious.'

Les was flattered by the attentions of a woman much younger than himself but also concerned by the age gap. He was confused too. He hadn't been looking for love. In fact, he had resigned himself to remaining single. Why would this pretty young woman want to be with him?

Amanda was drawn to the sensitive nature behind the public persona of Les – all twinkly eyes and dazzling smile. 'I had an image of Les as a game-show host and comedian but I found there was more to him than that. He knew more about acting than I did and he isn't a typical entertainer – he doesn't like being the centre of attention.'

John Bannister would say that it took him a while to realise what was going on. 'I didn't see it coming at all,' he says. When he became aware that he had lost Amanda to Les, John said he confronted him at a party and they almost came to blows. 'I grabbed him by the collar and said, "You'd better look after my girl." There was a bit of a scuffle and Lionel Blair pulled me away.'

Weeks before the end of the show's run John had another showdown. This time with Amanda. 'I said, "Why won't you tell me? What's going on?" She said, "I can't explain it. I just don't want to be married to you. Just listen to the Abba song 'Winner Takes It All', then you'll understand." And she stormed off. There was no goodbye, nothing.'

As Amanda's romance began to bloom with Les, the 39-year-old divorced father of one voiced his concern about their 17-year age gap and warned Amanda not to get too fond of him. She cheekily told him not to get too attached to her either. In his 2008 autobiography *Must the Show Go On?* Les recalled that he told her, 'I'm thirty-nine. You're twenty-two. There's no future for us.'

At the end of the summer season, when Les went to work in America and Amanda took a job on the perfume counter at Boots in Knightsbridge, west London, they were missing each other terribly.

'I went to LA for five weeks,' he later said. 'Ostensibly, it was about work and starting off my career in America but really it was getting away from a situation I didn't know whether I could control. I was worried – well scared, actually – about the age difference. Anyway, we ended up spending all our time on the phone – her bill came to £800. We'd only just met yet we needed to talk. I realised there was no point at all in staying in LA, so I came back and we went off to Disney World for a holiday. It was then we decided to give living together a try. I was very cautious – having been divorced once, I didn't want to rush it.'

True to his word, he would not make the ultimate commitment for three years.

Les was working on a cruise ship while Amanda was in Hamburg, Germany, appearing in the play *The Importance of Being Earnest*. One night, feeling lonely, he started drinking and, as melancholy set in, his thoughts turned to Amanda, how he was missing her, how good she made him feel and how he wanted to be with her – always.

Les picked up the phone and dialled Amanda's number. She recalled, 'It was Les, who sounded a bit the worse for wear. He blurted out, "Will you marry me?" I didn't know if he was serious, so I said, "Can I tell everyone?" He said, "Yes." And that's when I knew he meant it because he's such a private man.'

Les vividly remembers the moment when he threw caution to the wind and blurted out his heartfelt yearning. 'I was out of my brains when I asked her but I was very, very sure this was what I wanted. She was saying, "Can I tell everyone?" But I wanted to make sure my son Philip knew first. He shook my hand and said, "Congratulations!"'

Amanda was also excited professionally as she landed a bit part in the BBC soap *EastEnders* in 1994. 'I was only in it for six weeks, playing a stallholder named Carmen. I took over Sanjay's stall while he was away flogging jewellery.' Nevertheless, she thoroughly enjoyed being in the soap and, cheeky as ever, she had a novel thought as to how her character could return one day. '*EastEnders* was such fun. [Fellow actress] Patsy Palmer was lovely to me. The day I left [the fictional borough of] Walford I slipped a note under the producer's door suggesting Carmen should come back and that we should learn that her surname is Getme.'

Amanda and Les tied the knot in a Bournemouth church on 4 June 1995, with Lionel Blair and Su Pollard as ushers. Frank wasn't invited. The wedding was covered by *Hello!* magazine – which may have been seen as a harbinger of doom. The glossy celebrity mag has featured a long list of celebrity weddings over the years but, because so many of the marriages have subsequently failed, 'the curse of *Hello!*' has become a notorious phrase. Among those who have fallen prey to 'the curse' are Bill Wyman and Mandy Smith, Ulrika Jonsson and John Turnbull, Michael Jackson and Lisa Marie Presley, the Duke and Duchess of York, and Earl and Countess Spencer. But Les and Amanda were confident that they wouldn't be joining this list.

'It was the best day of my life,' Amanda recalled a couple of years later. '*Hello!* is said to be a curse on couples but we've beaten it and the wedding was wonderful.'

FOUR

MR & MRS

'I'm Mr Holden now. . .'
LES DENNIS ON MARRIAGE TO
AMANDA HOLDEN

Les Dennis had not been so happy in a long while. Amanda's infectious good humour and love for life seemed to have rejuvenated him. And she appeared comfortable in the loving embrace of a mature man. They may have been like chalk and cheese but here was proof that opposites attract. She called him 'Piglet' because 'he's all pink and lovely' and life seemed rosy in their three-storey 18th-century house in Highgate, north London.

'We may sound a bit gushy and silly, I suppose,' Amanda told the Scottish *Daily Record*. 'The other day someone was trying to find out what we row about. We don't, apart from normal things, like taking the dustbins out.'

Judith was delighted with her daughter's choice of partner. 'Amanda is very good for Les. I think they complement each other. Les can act the fool but he's got a serious side to him. She's given him a lot of confidence.'

Amanda appeared to like the fact that they were so different from each other. She helped to bring him out of his shell and he tempered some of her excesses. 'I'm still gobby, and put my foot in it and say silly things, but he's made me more careful,' she said. 'My best quality is that not a lot gets me down. I'm happy most of the time. Being with Les makes that easy.'

She said she loved playing the newlywed and all the publicity that came with being married to one of the best-known celebrities in the country. When asked if there were any plans to start a family, she replied, 'Well, my nan has knitted a shawl and Mum's brought the old family christening gown down – and they're telling me no pressure!'

The pair delighted in treating each other. For their second wedding anniversary, Les whisked her off to Venice, where they took a romantic gondola ride, had lunch in the stunning St Mark's Square and marvelled at the imposing Basilica. 'We walked and walked all day and then, in the evening, we sat in a beautiful restaurant beside the water. It was just fantastic,' said Amanda.

And for his birthday she took budding wine connoisseur Les for a weekend break to the beautiful former Cistercian residence-turned-hotel, Château de Gilly in Vougeot, France. 'It was the most fantastic three-day binge,' she said. 'It was lovely and very romantic. We ate lots, drank lots of wine and came back with crates of the stuff. I won't say how much it cost but we could have gone anywhere else for three weeks!'

Romance aside, there was no doubt that her marriage to one of the country's most popular entertainers, plus all the media coverage they were getting, boosted her career. Les had many showbiz friends and good contacts in the industry, and proudly introduced his vivacious young wife to them. Amanda loved meeting so many famous faces. This was the celebrity life she had dreamed of and there was no holding her back.

Amanda got a small role in a film called *Intimate Relations* in 1996, starring Julie Walters as a landlady who falls in love with her young lodger Harold, played by Rupert Graves. And it was Amanda who suggested Les play Harold's henpecked brother, Maurice. It was Les's first foray into acting and Amanda encouraged him.

'I knew I could do it but I was nervous because I was sure everyone was thinking, Is he going to be in his *Family Fortunes* mode?' said Les. 'Now I'd love to play a baddie in a soap. I'm from Liverpool and I wouldn't mind a crack at *Brookside* as a bit of a baddie like Trevor Jordache.'

A year later Amanda was one of the team in a new Channel Five comedy sketch show called *We Know Where You Live,* co-starring, among others, Sanjeev Bhaskar and Simon Pegg. It was a big job for Amanda, displaying her talent for comedy acting, and was to be a useful springboard to other work.

A guest role in the cop soap *The Bill* followed in an episode entitled 'Mr Friday Night', in which she played a mysterious good-time girl at the centre of a burglary investigation. She also became a regular guest in another comedy sketch show, this time on BBC2, called *Goodness Gracious Me*, starring Sanjeev Bhaskar and Meera Syal. She was going places fast, and Les was genuinely supportive and proud of his pretty, ambitious and talented wife.

In 1998 Amanda had a big break when she was cast opposite Caroline Quentin in a new BBC1 comedy series called *Kiss Me Kate*. The story centred on the daily routine of therapist Kate (Quentin), with Amanda playing her receptionist Mel.

With Amanda busy filming the series, Les took the opportunity to go on a school skiing trip to Canada with Philip. While he was away, Amanda was badly shaken up when she was involved in a car accident. She was driving Les's luxury 5-series BMW back from visiting her parents in Bournemouth when she careered into the end of a pile-up on the M3 near Basingstoke.

Thirty-two vehicles collided into the tailback of a crash that happened in heavy rain. Five people had to be taken to hospital. Luckily for Amanda, she just suffered a bit of whiplash and a pranged car.

'It was a horrible rainy day and the visibility was poor,' she said. 'I could see a car braking in front of me so I started braking slowly and then I realised the car was still getting nearer. At the moment I realised it had stopped, I slammed into the back of it.

'I felt so stupid. I was the last person. Bloody typical of me! You just feel awful. You sit there in the rain, and wait and pray that nobody crashes into you. Eventually, I was rescued by a recovery service. I was lucky I had no injuries. The car had several thousands of pounds' worth of damage but was repairable.'

Kiss Me Kate went out in May 1998, and was well received by critics and viewers. Meanwhile, Amanda had started work on another sitcom that was to further establish her as an accomplished comedy actress and also boost her image as a sex symbol. *The Grimleys* was an unlikely-sounding show set in the Dudley area of the West Midlands in 1975. The story centred on a teenager named Gordon (James Bradshaw) who was being bullied by his macho PE teacher Doug 'Dynamo' Digby (Brian Conley). Respite came from his friendly music teacher, played by former Slade frontman Noddy Holder. It had started as a pilot with Samantha Janus in the role of sexy English teacher Geraldine Titley, the subject of Gordon's schoolboy fantasies. But Amanda took over this role when it was commissioned as a series.

With Amanda on a fast-track route to stardom, the British press was fascinated by this celebrity 'odd couple'. He was the slightly naff old-style entertainer and she the pretty, young rising star. The biggest fascination was their age gap.

In one interview after another they were asked the same question: when would they start a family? 'I want girls,' said Amanda. 'I know that I'll have a girl because there are only girls in our family. Les has a son – eighteen-year-old Philip – but I believe it's my genes that'll come through.'

Never one to shy away from a direct question, Amanda dug herself deeper and deeper into a hole from which she would later have to try to emerge.

'I would love to have kids before I'm thirty,' she said. 'I would like two girls. I need shopping partners. My mother asks me constantly if I'm pregnant but I can't fit it in. I can't be pregnant for *Kiss Me Kate* and I couldn't for *The Grimleys* because it would have killed the storyline. They would have had to redesign my costumes or get me a big handbag.'

When they moved to a bigger house in Hampstead Heath, it fuelled new rumours that they were starting a family. And Amanda only fanned the flames. 'Our new home has too many rooms for two people and a dog, let's leave it at that,' she told reporters. 'My mum said that I had to fill the new house with children. So we'll just wait and see.'

Amanda had a good relationship with Philip, who was a regular visitor to their home. 'Les had been divorced for four years when we met, so there was no reason for Philip to have any problem with me,' she explained. 'We get on very well.'

As for Les, he was everything and more than she could

ever want – so she said. 'He has all the qualities a woman needs: he's funny, affectionate, generous, warm and so charming,' she gushed to the *Sunday Mirror*. Could there have been a more loved-up couple? In truth, work and her soaring success were driving her apart from Les – both physically and figuratively. Amanda was away in Manchester filming *The Grimleys* while Les waited for her. They were romantic when they were together and enjoyed the time they had when it was just the two of them but often had to keep in contact by phone. But perhaps even then Amanda was beginning to settle down into a routine when she was a bit too young for it.

Meanwhile, Les was becoming increasingly eclipsed by Amanda as she hogged the limelight. But he was typically modest and unassuming about it, and understood that she had to go for her career. Amanda was still outwardly playing the adoring wife but privately she was starting to notice the cracks in what they had presented as a perfect marriage. She had success in her own right.

By 1999 they had moved again – to a Victorian house in Primrose Hill, north London, which they shared with their cairn terrier Nobby. They also had a Victorian farmhouse near Hunstanton in Norfolk, where they enjoyed walking their dog and relaxing with visits to local pubs. 'Going there is like getting back to reality,' said Les. 'We just love being cut off from everything and able to enjoy each other's company.'

They had always insisted that age was never an issue

between them but Amanda eventually admitted that it was. 'Les doesn't act his age. He has the benefit of experience but he's very much on my level. In fact, I don't notice the age difference. The only thing that bothers me is that I sometimes think, Oh no, he's going to die before me; but then I could get run over by a bus. You never know what's going to happen.'

But, for the first time, she was starting to backtrack on the subject of starting a family. With her star in the ascendant, she said she knew that this was her time to focus on her career. This was the moment she had been waiting for to realise her dreams and she didn't want to waste the opportunity.

In another interview, this time in the *Sun*, she again said she wanted babies before she was 30. 'I've got to, I'm getting broody. And anyway, babies are a fashion accessory now. I've got to keep up with Posh Spice.'

But Amanda was beginning to realise that being a public figure meant that her exuberant, fun-loving and slightly risqué behaviour might not always be seen in the best light. 'People who know me know I'm quite camp and most of what I say is tongue-in-cheek,' she said. 'But when I read articles about myself . . . I come across as quite brash and rude. I am that as well but I really hope people don't think of me like that. I want people to see me as a nice girl who loves her husband and who has got lucky.'

Success had given her confidence but also made her more wary. No longer did she feel the need to please everyone or make them laugh all the time. 'I don't want to be the same sweet girl who came into the business at the age of twenty-two, and thought she could trust everything and everybody. Before, I always thought, I don't want to upset anyone. But now I won't take any nonsense from anybody ever again.'

Notably, it was Les who was ready to have a family, rather than Amanda. She denied he was putting any pressure on her but her intentions were clearly changing, as she went on to say, 'He's great about it. He just says, "As long as I'm still young enough to pick them up, I'll be happy." He knows I want children. I think I'm desperate for children deep down but I'm frightened of it changing me. I definitely want a child but I definitely want to keep working as well.'

Five years into her marriage, Amanda admitted that Les was something of a father figure to her. 'I do think most girls, if they have a good relationship with their parents, will look for the same qualities in their husbands as they have found in their dads. I think it's quite natural because that is the man who has had the biggest influence on your life since the earliest time you can remember. But it's not like Les is just a father figure. He's mother, father, lover, sister, all rolled into one.'

He had turned into a good cook and house cleaner too, while he was stuck at home for long periods and she was away filming. 'Les has become the most brilliant cook. I came home the other night and he had cooked roast sea bass with artichoke mash. It was gorgeous but the best thing about it was the kitchen was really tidy. When he first started cooking there used to be things all over the place and I would be running around after him, clearing everything up. But I said, "A good chef is a tidy chef, darling," and now he is.'

Amanda insisted that she didn't miss the single life and was happy to have settled down. But was she kidding herself? Was regret starting to set in?

'Lots of my girlfriends aren't married and they say they have a ball but I couldn't be out there again. Les is fun and immature sometimes but I know he's happy just being with me. Because he's older, he's already been there, seen it and done it, so I don't have to worry about him running off.'

Perhaps it didn't occur to her that Les might sometimes wonder about *her* running off. Despite overcoming his reservations about their age gap sufficiently to marry her, was there, at the back of his mind, the older man's perennial worry that his attractive and energetic wife would have more fun with a man closer to her own age?

In February 2000 Les joined the cast of the hit West End musical *Chicago*, playing Amos Hart, whose wife cheats on him and then kills her lover. Amanda thought it was a wonderful career move and Les had one of the musical's show-stopping numbers, 'Mr Cellophane'.

By April Amanda's thoughts on motherhood were taking a firmer turn and, in direct contradiction to what Les had earlier had to say about her ambition, she admitted the extent of it to the *People*. 'I have to say I'd sacrifice children for the sake of my career. My ambition is ruthless.'

That month the couple were rattled after they were burgled twice in quick succession. On the first occasion, the intruder rummaged through Amanda's belongings in their bedroom and stole some inexpensive pieces of jewellery, photos and Les's wallet. The second time, Amanda was at home with a friend when she heard the intruder, who fled when he realised he wasn't alone.

As the months went by, Amanda was displaying increasing signs that she was getting restless playing 'Mr and Mrs'. She publicly showed that she was still a young, vibrant and shapely woman when she posed in sexy underwear for *FHM* magazine.

'I'm proud of the way my body looks now,' she said. 'Every girl should do it at least once if they're happy with the way they look. I keep my sexy pictures on the mantelpiece. When I'm old, they'll be there to remind me of the good times I had. Who knows? I might be able to show my grandchildren!'

Meanwhile, she had started work on a brand-new comedy drama called *Happy Birthday Shakespeare*. Her co-star was Neil Morrissey.

FIVE

A PUBLIC AFFAIR

*'He's very cute but there's more going on
there than just his looks.'*
AMANDA HOLDEN ON NEIL MORRISSEY

Neil Morrissey had that rare quality of being able to charm both sexes. His love of beer and football meant that men wanted to drink with him in the pub, and women were captivated by his puppy-dog eyes, cheeky humour and 'bad boy' aura. This image was reinforced by the character he played in the popular TV comedy series, *Men Behaving Badly* – beer-swilling, football-loving, womanising Tony, alongside Martin Clunes. It was a persona that seemed to straddle his 'dual lives' on and off screen.

He also had a habit of falling in love with his co-stars.

He had met actress Amanda Noar while shooting the film *I Bought a Vampire Motorcycle*. They married and had a son, Sam, born in 1990. But Noar was shocked when after three years of marriage he fell in love with his co-star in his first big TV break, *Boon*. In this fondly remembered and warm-hearted drama series, Neil Morrissey played likable, easygoing biker Rocky, who helped private investigator Ken Boon (Michael Elphick). Liz Carling, in one of her first roles, played Ken's pretty assistant, Laura.

Morrissey was with Carling for seven years and they planned to marry. Then, in the middle of 1998, he fell for 30-year-old Rachel Weisz, his co-star in the TV film *My Summer with Des*. A devastated Liz had to move out of their home in London's Crouch End as his 'dream woman' moved in.

Two years later Rachel's career in Hollywood took off, following the success of the hit movie *The Mummy*. The long periods spent apart on either side of the Atlantic damaged their relationship and they finally split in March 2000. By the time he had started filming his latest TV drama, *Happy Birthday Shakespeare*, he was looking for love but not commitment.

'I'm an eligible bachelor, a mature man,' he said in interview, 'and I'm beginning to enjoy it. Why not? I don't think there's anybody who wouldn't want to be settled as they get older. But it's the nature of my life at the moment that I don't get a settled feeling. I'm trying to find a way to overcome my anxieties. Maybe it will happen. Maybe contentment will come.'

Amanda was amused to hear that she would have to romp in her undies with Neil Morrissey. *Happy Birthday*

Shakespeare was billed as a two-part romantic comedy, in which she played a tour operator named Alice who has an affair with her married coach driver, Will (Morrissey). Bored with what he sees as a dead-end job driving a tourist coach around picture-postcard sites of England, he yearns to buy a tearoom in 'Shakespeare county', Stratford-upon-Avon, with climbing roses up the wall, under the shadow of Anne Hathaway's Cottage.

Will met his wife Kate (Dervla Kirwan) on Shakespeare's birthday and so feels very attached to the great writer. When he meets beautiful new tour guide Alice, she persuades him to follow his dreams. And, during several overnight trips to Stonehenge, Bath and York, they embark on an affair.

'I play the mistress and Dervla the wife, so I didn't get to see much of Dervla,' Amanda commented at the time. 'Wives don't normally get to meet the mistress. We were fighting over the same man.'

Filming had got under way in Warwickshire in October 1999, immediately after she finished working on *The Grimleys*. Some saucy scenes, including sharing a Jacuzzi with Neil Morrissey, were not, she insisted, a problem to her. But then she had never been very bashful in showing off her body. After all, she *had* ridden naked on a motorbike through Bournemouth when she was 17 and stripped to her undies for *FHM*. 'I don't mind nudity,' she claimed before cheekily adding, 'but it does irritate me that you never see a decent nude shot of a man.'

For the past few years she had moved straight from one

TV series to another and the workload was starting to tire her. She had the urge to unwind and have some fun. She was also tired of being asked about having children and what it was like being married to Les Dennis. Feeling stifled, she was enjoying the breaks in between filming with her young and amusing co-star.

'For three weeks I was zooming around various English tourist resorts with Neil, living out of a suitcase and sleeping in hotels,' she said. 'It was quite knackering, filming four days a week and spending a lot of time travelling. My husband came up to Stratford and we booked into a hotel, so there were some compensations.'

Les had a cameo role as a character nicknamed the Milky Bar Kid, and met Neil and got on well with him on set. Les stayed a few days to film his scenes before travelling back to London.

Away from home, Amanda and Neil enjoyed the picturesque surroundings as they filmed in some of the most beautiful and charming locations in the country. They were also increasingly enjoying each other's company as the weeks went by. They found that they shared an infectious cheeky sense of humour, and an optimistic and upbeat approach to life. Amanda's tiredness began to dissipate as the shoot turned into one of the most pleasant that she had ever done. During breaks fellow cast and crew couldn't help but notice that Amanda and Neil would be giggling and whispering like two excited schoolchildren at the start of playtime.

'I quite like the gypsy lifestyle, and I had a few nice days out in Stratford and Stonehenge, although I have to admit that most of our sightseeing was done from inside the pub,' said Amanda in interview. 'Neil's a scream. He keeps up a constant stream of banter, which is invaluable on a job like this, where there's a lot of travelling and waiting around. He's actually a very clever and talented bloke. He's very cute but there's more going on there than just his looks.'

In just a few sentences Amanda had managed to list all the attributes that most women could wish for in the perfect man: looks, intelligence, talent and humour.

When filming came to an end, Amanda hardly had time to return home before she started filming a new series, a drama called *Hearts and Bones*. The story centred on a group of friends from Coventry who try to make lives for themselves in London. It co-starred Sarah Parish and Hugo Speer. Amanda was cast as Louise, a young woman whose world is turned upside down when she learns that her mum is dying from cancer. Amanda welcomed the chance to show that she could do gritty drama – even if it did make her cry.

'It was fantastic for me because usually everything I do is comedy. This couldn't have been more different. I had lots of emotional crying scenes and no gags at all. My character's very angry. She doesn't want to know about God or doctors and won't listen to her boyfriend.'

Amanda was feeling particularly good about her figure

around this time. In an interview with the *People* she remarked how pleased she was with her body and how she was enjoying a healthy lifestyle. 'I feel really good. I've been running regularly for a year and I've lost half a stone. It's brilliant, running. It tones everything up. I have cut out fat. I'm a vegetarian and don't smoke. I'm proud of the way my body looks now.'

Shortly after *Happy Birthday Shakespeare* was aired on 23 and 24 April 2000, rumours started to spread about the close relationship between the two former co-stars. By this stage the ever-busy Amanda was filming her latest TV role, a drama called *The Hunt*. The story was about a married woman who has a fling with a country squire.

While Les was appearing each night on the West End stage in *Chicago*, she rented a cottage near Yeovil, Somerset, where filming for *The Hunt* was taking place. Then, on 8 May 2000, the storm that had been brewing finally broke as the *Daily Mirror* carried a story with the eye-catching headline, A STAR'S ROMANTIC WEEKEND WITH LES DENNIS'S WIFE. Beneath it was a picture of the pair strolling, chatting and laughing together in the spring sunshine. The report said that they were enjoying an intimate getaway at the weekend as Amanda's five-year marriage was coming under increasing strain.

It described how they 'sniffed wild flowers they had picked from the side of the country lane – and lingered for an affectionate cuddle'. And it went on to tell how Neil had been getting cosy with Amanda in Somerset, enjoying long country walks and quiet drinks in the village pub.

In the photographs they did, indeed, seem like young lovers. Neil's surprise arrival in Somerset was the gossip of cast and crew, and they were instantly recognisable to the public too. What was going on? Surely they would be more discreet if they were having an affair. Perhaps she had already split from Les. Or could it all be a storm in a teacup?

In fact, Amanda had intimated to Neil that her marriage to Les was all but over. In truth, it was disintegrating fast because they were spending so much time apart. She had been filming three TV series in quick succession in the past six months and now he was on the West End stage every night.

They had managed to spend a weekend at their retreat in Hunstanton, Norfolk but work was soon calling them away from each other again. Now there were many miles between them once more. A week earlier Amanda had told a journalist, 'It's very, very difficult at the moment because he's working every night and I'm off working all day, often on location.'

And Les had also admitted to a reporter when Amanda was working on *Hearts and Bones*, 'At the moment it's hard because Amanda is working from seven in the morning to seven at night and I leave to go to the theatre at six in the evening, so we're just missing each other. But we do try to make sure that we set aside time for each other.'

But Les was shocked by what he read in the *Daily Mirror*. He knew Amanda was a natural flirt but, at the same time, he recalled the glowing and somewhat insensitive comments she had made to him about her co-star. After she had filmed love scenes with Neil for *Happy Birthday Shakespeare* she had told Les, 'I've got to tell you, Neil's a fabulous kisser. You see, like me, he's got big lips. It makes kissing so much nicer.'

Les had a sickening feeling that his long-held fear was true: Amanda was leaving him for a younger man. When Les failed to show up for that night's performance of *Chicago*, it added weight to the newspaper report.

A worried Les was racing to Somerset to find out exactly what was going on. With the rest of the press feverishly investigating this celebrity love-triangle story, a joint statement from Les and Amanda was released that read, 'We have a great deal of love for each other and, at the moment, we need time and space to discuss the situation, and would very much appreciate the understanding of the media.'

Some chance! This was one of the best stories they had had in a long while and they wanted every juicy detail.

Les and Amanda had a heart-to-heart in Somerset, where she admitted that she was having an affair with Neil. But, as he returned home on 10 May 2000, the matter had still not been resolved. That night he resumed his role in *Chicago* and received a huge cheer from the audience after one scene where he begs his stage wife to come back, saying that he loved her despite what she had done.

Neil's north London flat was besieged by the press but his amiable charm – not surprisingly – had deserted him. As reporters surged towards him when he came out of his front door, he gruffly told them to 'go away' before driving off in his BMW. And a grave-looking Les told reporters gathered outside *his* home, 'I want you to know I am doing everything within my powers to save my marriage.' Then, true to his nice-guy image, he added, 'I don't want Amanda to be made out to be the villain in this.'

But the public had already painted Amanda and Neil as the villains of this real-life soap opera. How could they do this to lovable Les? Amanda also looked to be feeling the strain as more and more about their private lives was being splashed across the newspapers every day. She was photographed arriving for work looking pale and hiding behind dark glasses, and she refused to talk to the press. A day later Les left his house looking much happier and assured reporters he was 'fine' before driving away. In stark contrast, Neil was in a thunderous mood when he started getting a spate of phone calls after a spoof advert appeared in the classified listings paper *Loot* looking for a gay flatmate and giving his mobile telephone number.

The advert read, 'Crouch End, N4, beautiful, clean double room and en-suite bathroom in a large flat, share with one gay guy, 34, £70pw incl.' An angry Neil, who did live in Crouch End but was actually 37, raged, 'I have had hundreds of calls because some prat put my number in *Loot*. I suppose I'll have to change the number.'

In the meantime, Amanda was still meeting up with him. They were spotted enjoying an intimate lunch at a London restaurant. By the weekend another joint statement was issued on behalf of Amanda and Les. It read, 'We reiterate that we still have a great love for each other but, at this time, we feel that space is needed, so we are going for a trial separation. Please respect our privacy so we can work through this. We are making no further comment.'

But there were other people willing to talk – including Frank Holden. 'It is absolutely heartbreaking for me as Amanda's dad to watch what is happening,' he told the *Sunday Mirror*. 'I just hope this is not the end of their marriage. I believe they still love each other and can pick up the pieces. Perhaps while they are apart they will change their minds. This split is all so sad. I last wrote to Amanda in February and she did not reply. That was very unusual for her. I knew instinctively that something was wrong – call it a father's intuition.'

He went on, 'I think Les is a lovely bloke. He has Scouse roots like me. I never thought the seventeen-year age difference between him and my daughter would be a problem. Morrissey may be a younger, more trendy bloke but I think she is better off with Les. I know from bitter personal experience how hard it is when a marriage breaks up. I think Les Dennis is a lovely guy. I was delighted when they got married. I'd love to help her now but I don't think it will happen and that is just so upsetting for me. After all, I'm her father and I always will be.'

Meanwhile, Amanda's mum, Judith, also spoke publicly about the scandal. She told the *Sunday Express* that she was hoping that some time apart would heal the rift. 'They still both think a lot of each other, they love and respect each other, but they need some time apart. A break is the best thing for them if they are to make this work.'

She also revealed how they were dealing with the situation in a mature and calm fashion. 'They're not fighting or shouting at each other but there is an awful lot of pain and hurt feelings. It's terribly sad. I love them both very much and I don't like to take sides. All I can say is I hope they will get back together.'

Meanwhile, Neil was denying that he had wrecked Les and Amanda's marriage. When asked by reporters if he felt responsible for the break-up, he replied sternly, 'No, I do not.' That evening he spent with a friend in Café Loco in Muswell Hill, north London, where he said his relationship with Amanda was over.

The day after their trial-break announcement, Les helped Amanda pack her suitcases and bags into her car as she prepared to move out of their home in Primrose Hill, and into a flat in nearby Hampstead. There was an embarrassing moment when, as he moved to kiss her on the cheek, she pulled away in front of the assembled press.

A few days later, Amanda arrived in her Range Rover

outside Neil's flat and they smiled broadly as he let her in. Two hours later he emerged to tell reporters, 'We're simply just good friends and we've been watching the FA Cup final together. That's all.' But the 'after-match analysis' must have been comprehensive because she was still there the following morning. Amanda hid her face as she was picked up by a chauffeur-driven car after lunch.

The drama took another turn when, four days later, Amanda and Les spent their first night together since their marriage break-up. They met for dinner after he came off stage in *Chicago* and were driven home shortly after midnight. But Amanda's behaviour just served to increase media speculation because, three days later, she was back at Neil's flat. Little wonder that Les's dignified silence was about to explode.

On 1 June 2000 Les attended the premiere party for his friend Ben Elton's movie *Maybe Baby* at London's Waldorf Hotel and launched a blistering attack on his love rival. 'Morrissey is a wanker,' he said. 'I'm glad he's a figure of public hate now. People have seen his true colours for the first time, what he's really like, and it isn't nice at all. I feel so full of anger towards him. It was a terrible thing that he did. I was very, very hurt by the whole thing. It's been extremcly difficult for me.

'I still love her, but I don't know what's going on at the moment. I'm just trying to move on with my life and get on with things. Nothing has helped ease the pain and I have to admit I'm now a single man again. We still talk all the time but that doesn't mean anything. Amanda really hurt me more than words can say. But what can you do? You just have to get on with life and make the best of it. I'm busy doing *Family Fortunes* and *Chicago* but it hasn't helped block things out. There's nothing I can do to forget what happened, it's all still so fresh in my mind.'

His old pal and fellow Liverpudlian, *Royle Family* star Ricky Tomlinson, gave him a big hug and Les, wearing his heart on his sleeve, insisted that he would find the strength to get through it. 'People have been really decent to me throughout all this. I'm in the public eye and, if someone asks me how I feel, I'm going to tell them. How do people expect me to feel – happy? But don't worry about me, I'm a big boy. I can get through this. I have to.'

On 4 June 2000 Amanda got away from it all with a holiday in Majorca with a female friend. She flew there just hours after celebrating her fifth wedding anniversary with her estranged husband.

A few weeks after her return she and Les announced that they were back together again – after they enjoyed a night out together watching a movie about an adulteress!

SIX

BACK TOGETHER

'Being persecuted for adultery –
I totally agree with that.'
AMANDA HOLDEN ON THE FILM *ANOTHER LIFE*

On 27 June 2000 Amanda Holden and Les Dennis announced that they were trying to patch up their marriage. 'It's early days but things are looking good,' she said. A rather downcast Les, clearly suffering from the strain, added, 'We just need a bit of space.'

They had enjoyed an evening at the cinema together watching *Another Life*, the true 1920s story of Edith Thompson, who was executed with her sailor lover after he had killed her husband. Showing her flare for dark humour, Amanda, now working on a second series of *Kiss Me Kate*, remarked, 'It was a great film. Being persecuted for adultery – I totally agree with that.'

Judith was delighted that they were back together. She told the *Daily Mirror*, 'Hopefully, this time it will work out. Obviously, I was upset with Amanda leaving Les. But Neil is not a bad man. Perhaps because of *Men Behaving Badly*, people assume he's that sort of person in real life. But he's kept his mouth shut throughout the whole thing and never said anything disrespectful.'

Judith told reporters, 'Unfortunately, Amanda had a distraction and was tempted. She hasn't had that many boyfriends and I felt it was a hiccup. Really, she's a loyal and stable sort of girl. The day before the news came out we were all together. It was so difficult because Amanda knew it was going to be in the paper the next day. She was upset. But since it has happened she and Les have had lots of talks. Even after they separated they never stopped talking and there was no animosity.

'Obviously, Les has been angry and upset – he has every right to be. But Amanda is an adult and I could only advise her. I think it was down to their being separated so much because they were working so hard.'

In August 2000 Les thought that dinner at The Ivy, a celebrity haunt in London's West End, with 71-year-old comedy actor Ronnie Barker and his wife, Joy, would be just the thing to cheer Amanda up. She put on a brave face.

Later that month they flew out on a make-or-break holiday to the South of France, where they rented a luxury villa in Cannes. It was here that they determined to make their marriage work and take the care to find time to be together. Les felt greatly relieved but it seems that Amanda knew she no longer felt the same way about Les.

Back home, Neil Morrissey received the bad news that the West End play he was appearing in, *Speed-the-Plow*, was forced to close due to poor ticket sales. He was taken aback when a huge wreath was delivered to the stage door addressed to him from a mystery 'sympathiser'. Shortly afterwards Neil spoke publicly for the first time about his affair with Amanda and dismissed the furore as a 'silly, crass story'.

'I suppose I've been seen as nice for too long,' he told the *Daily Express*. 'It was my turn to come under the cosh – to be made to look like a bad person. I am a bachelor. I'm not married. Why was it all my responsibility? I have no idea. I'm sure if Les wanted to say anything direct to me, he'd have phoned and said it. He never did. It wasn't for public viewing. It was a private matter. I don't want to get into the semantics of personal problems because it isn't just to do with me. It's too complex, and it's not my place to describe what was going on with Les and Amanda at all.'

In October 2000 Amanda revealed to the *TV Times* that she sought therapy after her fling with Neil but was told that she didn't really need it. 'You don't only go if you're mad, you know. You go if you feel you've got things to sort out. I went to see this really nice lady a couple of times but it just seemed like we had a lovely chat and I left thinking, Well, I feel great so I don't have to do that again. She said I was fine, basically.'

Her image as a scarlet lady was reinforced when she turned up at the prestigious National Television Awards in London later that month showing off her new red hair. 'Redheads have more fun,' she declared. 'It's permanent – I dyed my hair because I wanted a change.' But she was upstaged on the night by TV presenter Judy Finnigan.

Amanda and Les were on stage to present Judy and her husband, Richard Madeley, with an award for best daytime programme award for *This Morning*. As Judy leaned over to kiss Amanda, the top of her dress fell down revealing her bra to the packed audience and millions of TV viewers. And it was some time before she noticed! Amanda and Les both joined in with the laughter that filled the hall.

As Amanda neared the milestone of 30, she began to talk about ageing and how she had missed out on what could have been an exciting time as a carefree and single young woman in her 20s. And she admitted that she would have cosmetic surgery once she was no longer happy with her looks. 'If anything starts to droop or sag, I'm having the whole surgery thing. I'm really all for it,' she told *Shine* magazine in January 2001.

Since the split with Les, she had started having the occasional girly night out with her pals, including actress Sarah Parish. While Les enjoyed staying at home with Amanda, she increasingly wanted to go out – without him. Being out with her pals made her buzz.

'I've been married for seven years and we've always had couples as friends, so it's great to be going out with my girlfriends again. I love sitting in a bar, drinking and catching up,' she said. It was evident that the wild child was stirring within her again. She craved fun and excitement but time was running out. 'I've never been clubbing,' she said. 'I always used to say that I didn't like it but that was because I'd never even tried it.'

Amanda revealed that another reason she dreaded turning 30 was that people would expect her to behave like an adult. 'It's not just a vanity thing: you also know that you have to grow up. Loads of people have pointed out to me that it's good to be a successful woman in your thirties.'

Amanda's *Kiss Me Kate* co-star Caroline Quentin told *Heat* magazine that she had felt right in the middle of things during Amanda and Neil's affair, as she was friends with all three in the love triangle. 'It was just a stupid thing that happened. I think they all think that too now,' said Quentin, who had co-starred with Neil in *Men Behaving Badly* and was also a friend of Les. She found dealing with it very difficult. Caroline added that she thought it unfair that Neil got so much flak for the affair.

In early January 2001 Amanda and Les flew out to Los Angeles for a holiday together. There followed pictures of them in the newspapers looking genuinely happy and having fun together. He laughed as she cheekily groped his bottom in front of photographers at the airport. But then rumours began to emerge that Amanda had been secretly texting and phoning Neil back home. Just as Les was hoping that the spotlight was moving further away from their personal life, they were once more centre stage.

Amanda denied any contact with Neil, and stressed that she and Les were mending their marriage. 'There is no animosity between us but I don't want to see him at the moment because it would be a nightmare. Everything's very raw for Les and it's not fair. Things will die down and we'll be able to be friends again because that's how things started.' She went on to describe her year of hell as 'horrendous'. 'Les obviously loves me very much and I love him. He's certainly not the wimpy person he's been portrayed as in some of the newspapers. We have decided to make our marriage work because we have a history of seven years together.'

And she went on to indicate that *she* was the 'love rat' – not Neil Morrissey. 'I left my marriage for me, not for anybody else. And everybody involved knows that. I was in control of what I was doing and I still am. Neil was somebody who was there for me.'

Amanda talked about how she and Les were making a conscious effort to take time out together in order to repair their marriage. But should she have made a clean break? Was getting back with Les just going to make things even messier in the long run?

Meanwhile, Amanda was back on the box in a new series of *The Grimleys*. And Les, rather appropriately, was starring on stage in *Misery* at the Oldham Coliseum. In an interview with the *Observer*, he was in full sackcloth and ashes. 'I have to take account of the fact that, in a seven-year marriage, I might have made mistakes as well.' Les admitted that he leaned too much on Amanda for emotional support whenever he doubted his ability to entertain. 'I didn't believe in myself enough. And that can become difficult to cope with.'

Playing amateur psychiatrist, Les suggested that his lack of confidence stemmed from his father. Towards the end of March Amanda met up with Neil at the London private members' club, Soho House – the first time they had been seen together since their brief affair ended. But this time it was by accident and Amanda was quick to pour water on the rumours that they were seeing each other again. 'I was with friends and bumped into Neil Morrissey. Of course I said, "Hello," but I can categorically tell you that I have not restarted a relationship with him as suggested. My marriage to Les is strong. We are very happy.'

Meanwhile, *The Hunt* – in which she played an unfaithful wife – was being shown on TV, which did nothing to help her public image. But she made a public declaration of love to her husband after accepting an award from the men's magazine *Maxim* for Best Comedy Actress. Taking to the stage, she announced, 'Thank you to my lovely husband. I love you very much, darling.'

Ever ambitious, Amanda set her sights on having another shot at musicals. She had auditioned for her dream role of Eliza Doolittle in *My Fair Lady* on the West End stage but had lost out to former *EastEnders* actress Martine McCutcheon. 'I have attached my name to a play called *One Green Bottle* and, if I do it, it will be because the character in it gets to sing,' she said. 'It's something I've wanted to do for some time and I'd love to get back into doing musicals.

'I love Martine McCutcheon but, if she ever wants a rest from doing *My Fair Lady*, I'd be more than happy to take over the show. It's a part I've wanted for the whole of my life. I read an article about how Martine said she had practised for the part since she was six. Well, so have I. I'd gladly step in.'

Les, as ever, was quick to play Amanda's loyal and supportive husband. 'You should hear her sing,' he told the *Daily Express*. 'She's got a fantastic voice and she should use it more. You wouldn't believe how many scripts keep flying in for this woman at the moment.'

But it was Amanda's private life that kept dominating her professional one. During a break in filming the second series of *Hearts and Bones* she was snapped 'cosying up' to her co-star Hugo Speer outside the TV studios where they were filming their roles as lovers.

SEVEN

A SHOW OF COMMITMENT

'Things couldn't be better.'
AMANDA HOLDEN TALKING TO *TV TIMES*

In a series of intimate pictures splashed all over the newspapers Hugo Speer was seen draping his arm around Amanda. In others she was gently stroking his arm, they were nuzzling up together or she was kissing his brow. As the press began to get its teeth into another juicy instalment, spokespeople for both of the actors issued prompt statements denying any romance and saying that Hugo was a good friend, not only of Amanda's but of Les's also. Amanda added that, when the pictures were taken, they were surrounded by other people, so there was no question of any illicit affair. This time Amanda had nothing to hide.

In fact, it was Sarah Parish and Hugo who were in the first bud of romance. They had grown close after her broken engagement to theatre designer Fergus O'Hare. By the time the newspaper report had appeared Amanda and Les were on a month-long holiday in a villa in Tuscany, and Sarah and Hugo joined them there a few days later, where their relationship flourished. Amanda was happy to see her best friend in the first flush of love with her handsome co-star but it must have served to underline that such a feeling with Les had long evaporated. As their marriage rumbled along she became resigned to accepting what she had.

'I think you grow in relationships and, without making it sound like that's your lot, the phrase "as good as it gets" really means something to me now,' she told the *TV Times*. 'You realise you make mistakes.'

But the dynamics of their relationship had changed. She no longer saw Les through the eyes of a starstruck, ambitious 22-year-old and was bored with his 'old-school' celebrity pals. Now she had famous friends of her own. She was also a little embarrassed by Les's slightly naff image as a middle-of-the-road entertainer and game-show host. He had once appeared in a comedy sketch with Bobby Davro on a Cliff Richard TV show. It was a funny routine that had the audience laughing loudly but Amanda watched it grim-faced. A crestfallen Les realised that she was embarrassed by him.

True, the cheesy smile and quips were strictly for the camera and the private Les was very different. But, unfortunately, this side to his character meant that at home with Amanda he was prone to being introspective and downbeat. Amanda tried to be philosophical about it all, even though her heart wasn't in it, and she yearned for more out of her private life.

'I always think that each person becomes a teacher in a relationship,' she said in an interview. 'Very early on with Les I felt he was a teacher for me. We've been together for eight years now and halfway through that I definitely felt a change, that I became his teacher, helping him to take things a bit more lightly. My career's doing so well and Les is so successful but none of it would mean anything if we couldn't share it with each other.'

However, Amanda still felt the urge to get out and enjoy the big city while Les was far happier being at home – just the two of them. In fact, he wanted to move away from London altogether and live full-time in their Norfolk retreat. Not only would that mean he could enjoy a more peaceful, cosy and private life but he also thought it would help cement their marriage. However, while she genuinely loved spending weekends there, she didn't want it to become more permanent.

'I lived in a small village near Winchester until I was sixteen and had the best upbringing. But now I absolutely adore living in London,' she said. 'Les and I have the best of both worlds. Our cottage in Norfolk is our bolthole. As soon as we get any opportunity, we run there. In Norfolk you get your priorities straight. I don't wear any make-up or wash my hair. We just walk the dogs and enjoy pub lunches in front of an open fire. But I honestly don't think I could live in a village full-time. Les and I have discussed moving out of London but I couldn't do it. I love the buzz of all that's happening. I think being in a village would stifle me.'

In fact, it once nearly choked her to death! After a leisurely walk in the beautiful countryside they sat down for a picnic and Les – for a change – made her laugh so much that Amanda started to choke on her sandwich.

'We were in the middle of nowhere,' Les recalled. 'Not knowing the Heimlich manoeuvre [the first-aid technique to dislodge food by applying sudden pressure on the abdomen], I panicked. First I tried banging her on the back, then putting my fingers down her throat. Luckily, I had a bottle of water with me and, when she managed to swallow some, it was dislodged. But it was a terrifying experience. Amanda thought she was going to die and that's what I was afraid of.'

Whatever the truth about her private life, professionally she was soaring with more and more work coming her way. In September 2001 she appeared in the Sky One drama *Now You See Her*, playing con artist Jessica, who preys on wealthy men to fuel a lifestyle of holidays, flashy cars and designer clothes. But even workaholic Amanda was beginning to realise that she didn't have to take everything that was offered to her. By now she had the confidence in herself and her abilities to start being more selective. And she knew it was important for a long career.

'I'm learning to say no,' she said. 'As a jobbing actress I just worked, worked and worked. Being selective about what I do is a hard frame of mind to get into. It's scary too – although not as scary as being unable to sustain a career. Acting is a precarious business and, if I don't make the right choices, I could disappear and nobody would remember who I was.'

One of her choices was a new TV drama series called *Cutting It* about two rival hairdressers in Manchester. Amanda had taken the script with her on holiday to Tuscany, where she read it while lying beside the pool. It was proposed that she play the part of bitchy and scheming Mia, who puts Allie's noise out of joint when she turns up in Manchester from London to open a hairdresser's just a few yards away from hers.

Amanda loved the script and phoned her agent back home to accept the part. She also had an idea of who should play Allie. That person was lounging next to her – Sarah Parish. Although Sarah liked the idea, she felt that, because the pair had been in *Hearts and Bones* together so recently, she wouldn't have a chance. But she was delighted when she got the role alongside her best friend.

Before filming began, Amanda learned some of the tips of the trade by working with top London celebrity hairdresser Lino Carbosiero. 'I have spent the past couple of weeks working in a hair salon in London and have enjoyed every single minute of it,' she said. 'I was like the junior – I picked up rollers, held hairdryers, washed hair, but didn't do any cutting. And the funny thing is that I really enjoy it, just as much as acting. At the end of the week Lino said I had a job there if I wanted one!

'I've been styling everyone's hair, including my husband Les's. Now I don't think I would worry too much if roles started drying up for me because I've found something worth doing, which is just as fun.'

Fed up with the press dogging their every move, the couple made a stand when photos of them on holiday at their villa in Tuscany appeared in the *Daily Star*. They won a victory over press intrusion when Express Newspapers agreed to pay them an undisclosed sum for infringing their privacy.

As 2001 drew to a close Amanda went out in 'style' when she wore a dress made of cabbage leaves to help promote an anti-carnivore campaign by People for the Ethical Treatment of Animals. 'Next year be kind to animals and kind to yourself,' she said. 'Going vegetarian is good for your heart, good for your health and it's good for the animals.'

In the New Year Amanda learned she had another celebrity admirer. In an interview with the *Daily Mirror*, Simon Cowell, then a judge on the hit TV talent show *Pop Idol*, said, 'Everyone thinks I like blondes but I don't. I prefer brunettes. I chased Naima from [girl group] the Honeyz for years. She always turned me on. She is my dream woman. I'd make an exception for Amanda Holden. I bet she's really filthy . . . And Dannii Minogue.'

Amanda laughed at the comment but was secretly flattered. 'Filthy' may have not been the most chivalrous of adjectives but at least it implied that she was sexy and exciting.

By March that year Amanda and Les seemed full of the joys of spring, and made the biggest public declaration that their marriage was strong by renewing their wedding vows. They flew out to Las Vegas with four friends for the ceremony in the chapel at the Caesar's Palace Hotel. She wore a figure-hugging white trouser suit with a large white hat and carried a bouquet. Les wore a dark suit and a huge smile on his face. Later they went shopping, and he bought her some Christian Dior perfume and a suede cowboy hat!

The following month *Cutting It* was aired, and was well received by viewers and critics. 'The cast are terrific, the script sharp and witty,' said the *Express*. 'The scissors have never been sharper as the hairdressing world is revealed as a hotbed of sex and scandal,' drooled the *Sun*, while *The Times* described it as 'slick, stylish and pacey'.

By early May 2001 the show had already been signed up for a second series after pulling in 6.1 million viewers. And Amanda was excitedly singing its praises. 'I've never had so much response from people about any show I've done,' she said. 'Everyone wants to chat about it, which is very flattering. I judge everything on my mum and my nan: if something gets their seal of approval, I'm happy.'

Les also felt like a new start on a professional level

and announced his intention to quit the quiz show *Family Fortunes* after 15 years as host. But his move was prompted by his being asked to take a substantial pay cut as the show moved from an evening to a daytime slot.

Also in May, Amanda took a walk on the wild side when she travelled to the hills of Southern India with the wildlife charity the Born Free Foundation, to help publicise their campaign to rehome rescued tigers into the Bannerghatta National Park. Watching the tigers was a memorable experience for her. 'When you hear them roar, it sends a thrill right through you. You can't help but be bowled over. It's the most amazing sound. Then, as you watch them prowling about, you realise not only what dangerous animals they are but also how beautiful and awe-inspiring they are. Just the way they move is magical.'

Ever active, Amanda began work on a new sitcom with Harry Enfield called *Celeb*, based on a cartoon strip in satirical magazine *Private Eye*. Harry starred as ageing rock star Gary Bloke, married to cosmetically enhanced Debs, played by Amanda, who wore padding to increase her breast size and had her lips made to look as if they were pumped with collagen. The end result was, of course, way 'over the top' but it did make Amanda wonder whether she would resort to cosmetic surgery one day. 'I spend a fortune on creams and potions so, if something came out which might remove a line, I might be tempted,' she was reported as saying. 'I don't think I would go under the knife though. I don't think I would have a boob job unless I had kids and wanted them put back to where they originally were – I think that's fair enough.

'I do read all these articles on Botox and I would never say never. But I think actresses who have a lot are mad because you can't move your face.' (Botox is prepared from botulin and is used not only as a treatment for certain muscular conditions but also to remove wrinkles by paralysing the muscles in the face.) 'But acting is a youth-orientated game,' Amanda said. 'It's not just about your talent: it's about your physical appearance.'

Celeb marked a return to TV for Harry Enfield, who had been absent for a while. But neither viewers nor critics saw the joke. By the time the series had reached the screen *The Osbournes* – an amusing real-life fly-on-the wall series about rocker Ozzy Osbourne and his family – had made the idea redundant.

In stark contrast to *Cutting It*, the show got a mauling from critics. It was variously described as 'a tired excuse for a peak-time comedy', 'a satire that has taken on the easiest of targets and still missed' and 'just a fake imitation, and a poor one, of *The Osbournes*'. But Amanda defended it. 'I think the show is great – it's some of the best material I've ever done. To be honest, I have only read one good review and I haven't read any of the bad ones. I've had a fantastic time working with Harry and it doesn't matter what the critics say: the proof will be in the pudding when we see what the viewers think. I loved working on the show. Critics love to put the boot in – but that's the way of the business.'

Unfortunately, it didn't appeal to many viewers either and, to no one's surprise, was not commissioned for a second series.

As the affair with Neil Morrissey faded from people's minds Neil himself brought it rushing to the forefront when he talked about it to the *Sunday Mirror*. Ironically, while dismissing it as something from the past, he had brought it into the present once more by the very fact that he was talking about it. 'I never really spoke about it because I couldn't deal with the stuff which was going on and being slung at me. Everything went in the air,' he said. 'It was so unfair to be involved in some kind of slagging match, which is what it turned out to be.' He explained that, for him, it had been a bit of fun and then finished. He hadn't seen it as being behind anyone's back. He also stressed that it was in the past and he was no longer in touch with Amanda. He regretted the pain that it might have caused. 'I've so moved on.'

Now living with his TV-producer girlfriend of nearly two years, Georgina Hurford-Jones, Morrissey seemed surprised that the affair had caused so much publicity. 'The whole thing was brought up in a conversation with a friend of mine the other day. They said, "Your name's become synonymous with adultery." It's a terrible, terrible thing to be associated with. I haven't had that many girlfriends.'

Amanda, too, had moved on from Neil and turned her attention to an exciting business plan. Her idea was for her and Les to start their own production company. Les had little enthusiasm for the idea but was happy to go along with what she wanted.

Her comments to the *Evening Standard* clearly showed that the idea was all about benefiting her, rather than Les. 'The way we view it is that there are so many comedy actresses like me and there are about ten of them waiting to take over my part standing right behind me right now, so we have to have a plan.'

She also spoke of her desire to turn her back on light-comedy roles for those of more substance. 'I would say that I have almost come to the end of the road at the moment as far as being a comedy actress goes. I want to get away from happy-go-lucky girls and play strong, independently minded women. And I'm dying to go into production. I'm quite bossy, so I'd be quite good at it, I think.'

In her seemingly endless workload she began filming a new TV movie in the summer of 2002 called *Ready When You Are, Mr McGill*, in which she played the star of a cop drama called *Police Siren*, with Tom Courtenay as an extra given his first line and Bill Nighy as the director on the edge of a nervous breakdown.

Then in November 2002 Les was approached to be one of the housemates in the reality game show *Celebrity Big Brother*. He thought it through and, encouraged by his agent, who thought it might show a different side to his 'smiley, game-show-host' persona, he accepted the invitation. But his decision was to have shattering consequences.

Les entered the house on 20 November 2002 and his doom was sealed when the front door closed behind him. Once there the strain was plain for all to see and, when he emerged 10 days later, his wife would be gone.

EIGHT

TEN DAYS OF HELL

'She's cheering to keep me in here.'

LES DENNIS IN THE *BIG BROTHER* HOUSE

*B*ig *Brother* was the TV phenomenon that made the inane fascinating. A group of people live together under one roof with very little to do, every move and every utterance captured by TV cameras and microphones dotted around the house and relayed to an audience of millions.

With the participants stuck with people they may loathe, and with no privacy and nowhere to hide, it often proved to be an experience of increasingly high emotions as snipey remarks dissolved into tears, tantrums and slanging matches. Some coped better than others as the days rolled on.

In the first celebrity edition of the show in 2001 – which was a part of *Comic Relief* – TV and radio broadcaster Vanessa Feltz had famously suffered a meltdown. She had just recently divorced her husband, with whom she had two daughters, after 16 years of marriage. During the break-up she suffered angst and lost four stone in weight. It came on top of her mother Valerie's death from cancer a few years earlier and also the axing of her BBC chat programme, *The Vanessa Show*, after it was discovered that some actors posed as guests and the show was not renewed.

After a few days in the house, which she was sharing with the likes of Anthea Turner, Claire Sweeney and eventual winner Jack Dee, she began acting strangely. Dressed in a silk leopard-skin dressing gown and sunglasses, she chalked the words 'incarcerated, diffident, disparate, frustrated' on the table. She later described her bizarre actions as 'a mix of angst, suffering and personal disaster. It was a rough stage of marital upset. I didn't deal with it too well. It was like being stuck in a lift and not being able to get out.'

Entering the *Celebrity Big Brother* house appeared to be an odd decision for Les to make, given his private nature, shyness and sensitivity. Living under the glare of the lights and cameras watching the incumbents' movements 24 hours a day seemed as if it would be his idea of hell. The other celebrity housemates were comedian Sue Perkins, presenters Melinda Messenger and Anne Diamond, and musicians Mark Owen and Goldie. An hour before they were due to enter the house each of the celebrities was given the chance to say goodbye to their family and friends in a separate room. Amanda, who had been filming the second series of *Cutting It* in Manchester, managed to travel down to Elstree, Hertfordshire, where it was taking place, to see Les off but she failed to put her edgy husband at ease. In fact, she made things worse.

'Don't worry, darling,' she announced to the room. 'I'll definitely have your voting number on redial to keep you in. I'll enjoy a bit of freedom.' There were a few nervous laughs but not from Les. It may have just been her wicked sense of humour but, given what had happened in the past, Les was struggling to see the funny side.

But Amanda had an audience and was on a roll. 'And you know that I won't be able to get away from filming to greet you as you come out. The Beeb have got me on an extremely tight schedule. Not even sure I'll be able to watch a lot of the show. Be thinking about you though, darling.'

More nervous laughter was followed by an awkward pause, which was filled by Les's agent, Mandy, who said that there was a strong rumour that Endemol, the makers of the show, were going to introduce an extra, secret housemate. Amanda was the first to respond and jaws visibly dropped as she said, 'Wow! Wouldn't it be amazing if it was Neil? You two in the house. That would be fascinating.'

As everyone started to leave, Les had a final hug with Amanda and whispered in her ear, 'Why the fuck did you say that?' She replied, 'Oh, darling, it's only a joke. Lighten up.'

But, for Les, it was the worst possible send-off. On his first night inside the house he was already starting to get emotional because he was missing Amanda. 'It's about this time of night that you want to ring home,' he told his housemates.

Meanwhile, Amanda, back in Manchester filming *Cutting It*, commented, 'All those in the house seem to be getting on well with Les – I just hope he wins. It's very frustrating that we can't ring each other.'

But Les wasn't coping well. The press had nicknamed him 'Les Miserable'. Showing signs of missing Amanda, he had a boozy evening session, drowning his sorrows.

Clearly still haunted by Amanda's affair, he got a lot off his chest after five days in the house when he told the housemates, 'To get over something like that was extremely difficult for us, especially with the coverage it got. But we managed it and some people think affairs can even make you stronger as a married couple. Younger people seem more accepting of affairs.'

He even suggested that their relationship could be seen as a role model. 'In our business, where marriages don't work, something happened and we got back on track. Shouldn't we be seen as pioneering? As with any relationship, these things happen. But it's another thing to get over the celebrity spotlight. We're still together and now we're not allowed to get over it. Whenever she's in the company of another bloke, there's a media frenzy.'

In full flow, Les continued to share his private thoughts

and worries to a fascinated TV audience and rather embarrassed housemates. 'I fell in love with Amanda at first sight. We haven't got kids, and can just stand up and leave when we want. But we are two people who choose to stay with each other.'

Again, he took the opportunity to stand up for Amanda and accused her critics of having double standards. 'If it had been me, they would have said, "OK, Les, that's fine, good for you. Hey! Les the lad." But she's had to endure two years of shit.'

Take That singer Mark Owen tried to lighten the tone by joking that his best chat-up line was, 'Do you know who I am? I'm Robbie [Williams'] mate.' But Les was not to be put off and he related how they had first met and fallen in love, and the reservations he had had about their age difference. Amanda was watching on TV in Manchester with Sarah Parish and her *Cutting It* pals as Les went on to reveal how the death of his mother and father before he was 30 affected him. With tears in his eyes, Les recalled the evening he went to stay at a friend's house without leaving his parents a contactable phone number. When he awoke the next day he found out his father had died.

Les was nominated for eviction from the house but survived when viewers voted Goldie out instead. He may have been missing Amanda but, tellingly, the day after Goldie's eviction he revealed that Amanda wanted him to stay in the house. 'She's cheering to keep me in here, not to see me again.'

When asked by Melinda Messenger whether he would like to start a family, glum-looking Les replied, 'Yeah, I think so when the time is right. Men are fertile but there is that line in *When Harry Met Sally* when Sally says, "It's OK for men, Charlie Chaplin had kids when he was seventy." But then Harry says, "He was too old to pick them up."'

Things took a new turn as he started talking to the chickens. He angrily accused *Big Brother* of secretly stealing eggs from the chicken coup when he went to check them. He branded them 'bastards' and screamed at the cameras to stop following him around. After he had calmed down he murmured to the chickens that they were his only real friends.

The kitchen taps were next to feel the heat of his wrath when he was unable to turn them off properly. And, in an insightful comment to Melinda about the disparity between him and Amanda, he said that men 'are in crisis' and 'haven't got a clue what women want. Amanda runs to listen to Robbie Williams and I walk to listen to *Woman's Hour*. What's that all about?'

In another late-night chat he talked once more about Amanda and the guilt he felt at walking out on his young son. He admitted to his housemates that he had undergone three years of therapy after the end of his first marriage to Lynne, and the deaths of his parents and comic partner Dustin Gee, within three black years.

'My most difficult decision in life was to decide to leave

my first family, with a ten-year-old boy between us. I walked away from the house but I never left him. I have always been there for him. I beat myself up about that. I have huge guilt.'

After a heavy night's drinking and soul bearing Les decided it was time for a swim – at 2am. A concerned Melinda suggested that they should retire to bed and all go swimming later but Les was having none of it and got into the pool in his pyjamas, still holding a glass of wine.

After a while, he started questioning his actions. 'God, what am I doing? I'm here on my own and now I'm even talking to myself.'

Later Anne Diamond told him he was spiralling out of control and Sue Perkins advised him to enter the 'Diary Room' to talk to Big Brother. Les admitted to Perkins that he 'wanted to be liked'. Increasingly irritated and bored with his behaviour, Sue said in the Diary Room that he was desperate for approval.

Les shed more tears when he was forced to choose two housemates for eviction and later made a bizarre remark in the Diary Room when he confessed, 'I think I've been performing.'

Meanwhile, speaking on Capital Radio, Amanda pleaded with listeners to keep her husband in the house longer – a comment that could be interpreted in more than one way. 'Please vote for my husband because I'm working in Manchester so I don't get to see him anyway and I'm missing him by not talking to him on the phone,' she said.

'But I am actually having quite a peaceful week, so let him stay in until Friday.'

In another ambiguous comment she said that she was annoyed with him for saying that he thought he had been performing, insisting, 'He's absolutely being himself.' The public was left wondering whether it was all an act from Les or whether he was really like this at home.

Les emerged as runner-up on the show, behind Mark Owen. While all the other housemates had their nearest and dearest there to embrace them as they emerged from the house, Amanda – as she had intimated – didn't turn up.

Years later, in his autobiography, *Must the Show Go On?*, Les explained with brutal honesty why he had decided to take part in the show. 'There was nobody beating a path to my door to offer me any new and exciting projects, so my agent Mandy and I decided that we had to raise my profile,' he wrote. He explained that, although he never really liked the original *Big Brother*, he'd got into the idea of the celebrity version after seeing *Comic Relief* do their version. 'Looking back, I can see that one of the reasons I went into the house was because I was still driven by the fear that had always haunted me, that one day I would lose it all, and end up unknown and poverty-stricken.'

NINE

THE FINAL STRAW

'The parting is amicable.'
AMANDA HOLDEN AND LES DENNIS
IN A JOINT STATEMENT

Once more Amanda Holden was miles away – in Manchester, still filming *Cutting It*. So, instead of her being there in person as Les came out of the *Big Brother* house, he was shown a video tribute from her telling him how proud she was of him. Despite the warm words, it was oddly impersonal.

With Amanda flanked by two of her *Cutting It* co-stars, there was much giggling between them before she eventually said, 'At this point we have no idea where you've come but you've done so well to get through to the last three. You've been very brave. You have been extremely honest and I'm really looking forward to seeing you.'

At the press conference afterwards Les was putting on a brave face and was at pains to explain his wife's absence.

'She's on a night shoot. I knew you guys were going to ask me about this. We are both in a business where this happens.' He added that he planned to head up to Manchester the following morning to be with her.

Of his time in the *Big Brother* house, he attempted to explain his behaviour to the show's presenter, Davina McCall. 'In the eighties, people in light entertainment were seen as a bit naff. I didn't want to be like that. When you have a game show for fifteen years, everyone sees a cheeky, smiley Les. That's not the real deal. I wanted to show that.'

But the side of Les that he showed to an increasingly surprised public was not universally understood. Les did not travel to Manchester as he had said, and he told several newspapers and TV shows that the reason was that he was learning his lines for his new role in the BBC medical drama series *Casualty* – as dodgy garage owner Pip Benson.

But as November passed into December Amanda still hadn't returned home to see Les and he hadn't been to see her. The media were in a frenzy about the state of their marriage. There had even been a report that Amanda had been in contact with Neil Morrissey while Les was in the house. It wasn't true but it added fuel to the speculation.

Once more Les had to put up with a group of reporters outside his house and he irritably shouted at them that he would be seeing Amanda later in the week because they were both busy working. But Les was a worried man. He was later to admit that, when he came out of the house and was told that Amanda had taped a video message for him, his heart was filled with dread because she 'couldn't be bothered to do it live'. He was also upset that she was with her *Cutting It* co-stars and not alone.

As 'Amanda watch' occupied the press Amanda's sister, Debbie, offered Les some support. After a walk in the winter sunshine together they had lunch with friends. Amanda finally returned home 15 days after Les had left the *CBB* house – but she wasn't staying long. She had to return to Manchester to continue filming. Les, too, was pleased to get out of the house as he travelled to Bristol to film *Casualty*. But was this just 'ships that pass in the night' or was their marriage well and truly scuppered?

Once in Bristol Les was seen in a hotel bar by a reporter from the *Sunday Mirror*, who wrote a devastating account of what happened next. The story told how they had struck up a conversation while Les was in the middle of dealing with the fallout. An emotional Les opened up his heart, saying that he got very upset about what he read about himself and Amanda in the papers. The female reporter claimed that he was drinking heavily, asked her for 'a cuddle' and suggested they run away together. He told her that he had 'reached a crossroads' and didn't know where his life was going. The following day Les lunched with some of the *Casualty* cast and the journalist reported seeing him again and that he remarked he felt 'fragile'. He said that he was planning to spend Christmas with Amanda and her parents.

The bombshell appeared in the *Sunday Mirror* in sensationalist form. If their marriage had not already ended in Amanda's mind, it certainly had now. It was the final death blow. With reporters trailing Les and Amanda's every move, they were both photographed out in London eight days before Christmas – but they were not together. Les was seen leaving the TV studio of Five's *Chris Moyles Show*, which he was co-hosting for the week, quickly getting into a car to dodge reporters' questions. Just a few minutes away Amanda was having a pleasant dinner at The Ivy with her *Cutting It* co-stars Sarah Parish, Angela Griffin and Lucy Gaskell.

The few words spoken between the two since his return from Bristol were just to confirm that the marriage was well and truly over. Les spent Christmas in Liverpool with his two sisters while Amanda invited her family to spend Christmas Day with her at home, where she told mum Judith and stepdad Les Collister about their marriage split.

Two days later Amanda's and Les's spokespeople released a joint statement saying that their seven-year marriage was over. It read, 'The parting is amicable. There are no other parties involved, and they are and will remain close friends.'

Once they had made their decision they did, indeed, behave amicably towards each other. 'It's very sad,' said Amanda. 'We've been together for ten years and we've tried hard to make our marriage work. I have the most enormous love and respect for Les.'

And Les remarked, 'Amanda and I have had a good marriage and I have no regrets. Sadly, we've grown apart and we both feel it's time to move on. I wish her good luck in all that she does in the future.'

Deciding Amanda needed cheering up, Sarah Parish arranged a five-day break for the pair of them, along with three other girl pals, at Barcelona's five-star Hotel Arts.

A day later Les also got away from it all when he boarded a flight from Heathrow to Johannesburg, heading for northern KwaZulu-Natal, where he stayed with his friend Paul Whittome, owner of the Hoste Arms in Norfolk, at his holiday home. As he flew out an upset Les told reporters, 'I don't want to talk about my marriage. She can do what she wants. She can tell the press what she likes but I don't want to talk about it, really.'

Meanwhile, in Spain, Amanda was determined to enjoy herself. Although the end of her marriage was naturally upsetting, it had not been unexpected. Now she was free and single once more and able to do all the things she wanted without having to worry about Les. The towering Hotel Arts rises majestically from the shores of the Mediterranean Sea, overlooking miles of beaches and the grand vista of Port Olympic, and provides a luxurious experience for guests. The modern steel-framed construction contains more than a thousand works of contemporary Spanish art.

A giant steel fish sculpture hovering by the swimming pool is an eye-opening sight for new arrivals. The opulent and stylish interior has a top-range spa, and several restaurants and bars, which Amanda and her pals took full advantage of. The rooms have a modern, straight-line look in cream and brown, with panoramic views over the sea and the city of Barcelona, where they indulged in frequent shopping trips as well as sightseeing and, later, drinking and chatting back at their hotel.

On New Year's Eve Amanda wore a gold hat and comical false nose and glasses as they quaffed champagne in the hotel bar, while Les was drinking bubbly at a private party on a beach near Durban, overlooking the Indian Ocean. As reporters from British newspapers lurked around, trying to talk to or get pictures of Les, Paul Whittome told them that Les was not miserable but had 'a tremendous smile on his face'.

He added, 'Les is a great guy and a good buddy. We have been friends for about ten years and, after I heard about the split, I called him and asked him to come over. It's the first time he's been here and he's really enjoying it. He's getting on with his life – he's that kind of guy. Les is in good form. He's relaxed and having a wonderful holiday.'

But as time wore on Les was to prove that he was not 'that kind of guy' at all and found it very difficult to carry on life without Amanda.

Amanda flew home on 2 January 2003. A few days later Sarah Parish was interviewed on ITV's *This Morning* and spoke about their Spanish holiday. 'Amanda seems to be holding up all right but it's proving to be very difficult for her. It doesn't help when the break-up is in the papers – divorce is very private. But it was a great New Year.'

Some months earlier Amanda had bought a flat in St John's Wood, north London, which she said was 'an investment'. It was here that she moved after returning from Spain. But the apartment barely had time to get warmed up before she was heading back to Manchester to continue filming *Cutting It*.

Meanwhile, Les landed a role in the ITV soap opera *Crossroads*. After he had talked in the *Big Brother* house about his therapy another heavy dose of irony saw him cast as smooth-talking psychiatrist Dr Richmond.

In positive mode, he remarked, 'I don't want everybody to feel sorry for me. I'm just trying to get on with life. It's the beginning of a new chapter for me.'

But by now the public were realising that he just couldn't let go of the past, no matter what he said. He announced that he was doing a one-man theatre tour called *An Evening with Les Dennis*, starting in April, in which he would discuss all aspects of his life, including, of course, Amanda.

Les, who had confessed to spending his evenings alone watching movies and eating takeaways, said he was making the tour to show people that he could joke and smile after his bad time on *Celebrity Big Brother*.

In contrast, Amanda was living very much for the day and throwing herself into the single life with a round of nights out with her girl pals.

TEN

THE SINGLE LIFE

'I am living the life I want to lead now.'

Amanda Holden on the single life –
and shopping

Never one to sit and mope, Amanda was making the most of her life. Now was the chance to 'reclaim' some of her lost youth by partying hard. The wedding of her hairdresser friend Lino Carbosiero on 1 February 2003 at London's Park Lane Hilton Hotel included such celebrity guests as Tamzin Outhwaite, Jane Horrocks, Anna Friel, Isla Fisher, Sacha Baron Cohen and Martine McCutcheon.

After wedding vows were exchanged the guests relaxed and chatted animatedly at the lavish reception. But, according to reports there was a bust-up when Martine asked Amanda why she didn't like her.

Guests were puzzled by the fracas but there was some rivalry between them. Eight years earlier when Martine joined *EastEnders* as cheeky Tiffany she quickly became one of the show's most popular characters and the high-profile role turned her into a household name.

Amanda had landed a minor role of stallholder Carmen a year earlier and some journalists speculated that she might have wanted her part to be developed in a similar way. And Amanda and Martine had both auditioned for the West End stage role of Eliza Doolittle in *My Fair Lady*. When illness forced Martine to cancel several performances, Amanda was reported as saying she would happily take on the role if Martine no longer wanted to do it.

A few days after the wedding Amanda was back in the news when a secret lover was splashed all over the *News of the World*. It told how she had been romancing Danish pop singer Thomas Barsøe and that they had been lovers since Christmas 2002. In later comments he said they had, in fact, been intimate since the summer, when she was still with Les. But Amanda angrily denied it and said that she had met the 22-year-old singer on only one occasion – at a party at Kensington Roof Gardens following a charity football tournament in Chelsea.

Meanwhile, Les had another woman in his life. To his surprise, he had met PR Leoni Cotgrove while in a pub near his home. Leoni, who was based in Madrid, had come home to visit her mother, Veronica, one of Les's neighbours. Like Amanda, blonde-haired Leoni was 17 years his junior but Les felt comfortable with her. She lent a sympathetic ear to his worries but also cheered him up. They had a string of dates before she returned home.

Les flew out to Spain to see her in February and they booked into a hotel and made the most of their time together before she was due to go back to work and he returned to London. By this stage the press had got wind of the romance and a picture appeared of the pair of them strolling on the beach, kissing and cuddling. Les was smiling broadly – a rare sight of late. He had found love with Amanda when he wasn't looking for it. Had the same thing happened again? 'We are just enjoying a lovely holiday together,' he told a reporter from the *Sun*.

Amanda was genuinely pleased that he had found a new love because she had been worried about his not finding a girlfriend. She and Les had kept in touch, and he had told her about Leoni.

While Les was lapping up the Spanish sunshine she was in Manchester filming *Cutting It*. But Amanda was having a whale of a time, living near to her co-stars Sarah Parish and Angela Griffin. They were all single – Sarah had split with Hugo Speer – and they shared Amanda's love of fun and parties. And, when not going out, Amanda would invite the girls to her flat. On one occasion they had a special party there to mark the first night of the new series of *Footballers' Wives*.

Amanda loved this camp TV drama about the platinum-blonde and platinum-credit-card-loving wives of the famous footballers from fictitious Premier League side

Earls Park. The bitchy battles between the wives made for some amusing put-downs and viewers lapped up the memorable catfights between arch antagonists Tanya Turner (Zöe Lucker) and Amber Gates (Laila Rouass).

There were also girly nights in for her other favourite show, *Sex and the City*, starring Sarah Jessica Parker as Carrie, leader of the pack of four female New Yorkers who regularly meet to gossip about their sex lives. 'I make very good cocktails and we all wear negligees and our best underwear, and watch it together,' said Amanda like an excited teenager.

At the weekends she would return to her home in north London and carry on enjoying the nightlife, often continuing where she left off with her *Cutting It* friends, Sarah Parish, Angela Griffin and Lucy Gaskell, who all lived in London.

Men, it seemed, were off the menu. Arriving for the Royal TV Society Awards, she told reporters, 'As far as blokes go tonight, all I'm interested in is seeing what they're wearing. I've had enough now, and just want to let my hair down and go on holiday where no one will find me.'

Her 32nd birthday on 16 February 2003 was another opportunity for a girls' night out – in style. She took her actress friends Sarah Parish, Lisa Faulkner, Nicola Stephenson and Angela Griffin to the chic London restaurant Hush. Located in a quiet and secluded courtyard in Mayfair, it is far from 'hushed' inside. The modern and stylish interior buzzes with diners, and waiters scurry around attending to their needs. But, despite the bustle, Amanda's table attracted much attention. It was decorated with pink balloons and the birthday girl shrieked with delight as the girls gave her pink champagne, a special-edition pink Yorkie bar and frilly pink knickers!

In recognition of her love of shoes and shopping they also arranged for a cake to be made in the shape of a cushion on top of which rested an iced silver Manolo Blahnik strappy shoe. They ended the evening by going clubbing.

In an interview with the *Mail on Sunday* Parish talked about her great friendship with Amanda. 'Amanda and I are not needy around each other. I think that helps friendships because you never feel obliged to do anything. I might not speak to Amanda for a month but, when we do talk, we pick up from where we left off. It's no big deal. With some friends, you feel you have to apologise if you haven't spoken to them for a while and I find that difficult.'

Although the press was constantly trying to link Amanda romantically with a new man, she felt uncomfortable at the thought of being on the dating scene again. It was something she hadn't done since she was little more than a teenager, before she had met Les Dennis at the age of 22.

'If I'm honest, I'm a bit nervous. I know dating can be a bloody nightmare,' she told *Red* magazine. 'I'm linked to about three men a week. But when I'm out, I'm with girlfriends putting the world to rights over a nice bottle of champagne. This Valentine's Day all I opened was a gas bill. But I'm more than surviving: I'm really living and it's great.'

Her biggest love at the moment was shopping! She had always enjoyed buying clothes and now she was in overdrive. 'I'm shopping like hell, it's a real outlet for me. I am living the life I want to lead now.'

In March 2003 Amanda – who had always dreamed of a transatlantic career – went to Los Angeles to meet up with her US agent and be introduced to some influential people. She stayed at the plush Four Seasons Hotel, which had the benefit of being just minutes from the 'shopper's paradise' of Rodeo Drive and Robertson Boulevard. And, to her delight, the hotel provided courtesy cars for guests to take them there and bring them back whenever they were ready.

Successful as she was, Amanda still wanted to make it in the States and never took no for an answer. And she would keep going back over the years to try again.

The following month she got the get-away-from-it-all holiday she was after as she and Sarah Parish headed to Barbados. They stayed at the idyllic Turtle Beach Resort, located on a 1,500-foot stretch of white sandy beach. Here they whiled away their days sunbathing, strolling along the beach or swimming, either in the sea or the resort's swimming pool. They also enjoyed wandering through the lush tropical gardens.

Meanwhile, Les revealed that his favourite place in the world was Norfolk. 'I love Barbados, Mauritius is wonderful and Tuscany has amazing scenery. But my favourite place has to be Norfolk, where I have a holiday home. There's this beach called Holkham – it's stunning.'

Back home Amanda began work on a new TV comedy series with Jamie Theakston called *Mad About Alice*. They played an estranged married couple who realise they are still in love with each other. But things are complicated because Doug now has a pretty surgeon girlfriend and Alice has met a hunky surfer. Not surprisingly, the press was looking for signs of a real-life romance between the co-stars and the *Daily Mail* reported that they had been seen 'kissing passionately at a nightclub'.

But Amanda laughed off suggestions that they were in a relationship, saying, 'Jamie's a lovely bloke but we're definitely not dating.'

In May 2003 Les started his one-man touring show, *An Evening with Les Dennis*, but few people took up the invitation. Ticket sales were disastrous as he found himself playing to half-empty auditoriums. Or even less. At his opening date at Swindon's Wyvern Theatre only 250 of the 617 seats were filled. At one point he ordered a pizza on stage, joking that there would probably be enough to go round for everyone present.

Once again Les only proved that he was still infatuated with Amanda. Towards the end of the evening he bizarrely held up a photo of himself and Amanda on their wedding day, and said, 'At some point I married this lady. She's a lovely lady. Our relationship has ended but don't believe everything you read. She is great.' Their two dogs, he said, were 'in joint custody, both loved, and both come between mum and dad'.

The following Saturday Amanda was a guest on *Parkinson* and she told the chat-show host that she still loved Les, even though they were getting divorced, and that she phoned him every day. When Michael Parkinson asked what she believed people thought of her, she replied, 'Well, a nice word would be "minx",' adding, after some thought, 'or "slapper".' It got a big laugh from the audience and went some way to softening any harsh perception of her.

Her relationship with Neil Morrissey was, she said, a 'terrible mistake' and, looking back, she couldn't believe that she thought they would be able to share country walks together and not get caught.

Amanda also admitted, for the first time, that getting back with Les was another mistake. 'I shouldn't have gone back but I just didn't want to get divorced.' She added that she was happy being single for the first time since she had been 16 and that it would 'take a very brave man to love me'.

Les continued to perform to sparse audiences. His show at the Becks Theatre, Hayes, Middlesex, was even more disastrous, when only 60 of 600 seats were sold. But he wasn't the only one feeling unloved. At a charity event at London's Great Ormond Street Hospital Amanda bent to kiss a four-year-old boy patient but he turned away, which caused her to mumble, 'That seems to happen to me all the time at the moment.'

That May the second series of *Cutting It* went out and the *Sun* praised her portrayal of scheming Mia, stating, 'Minxy Mia (a wonderfully catty Amanda Holden) is shaping up to be the biggest TV bitch since *Dynasty*'s Alexis.'

Still hankering for a West End musical, Amanda was excited when the producers of a new stage version of the hit movie *Thoroughly Modern Millie* invited her to fly out to New York to watch the show and audition for the lead role when it came to London.

Thoroughly Modern Millie, set in the 1920s, was originally a hit movie in 1967, with Julie Andrews starring as feisty flapper Millie, who aims to marry a wealthy man but eventually finds true love instead. Amanda watched the show enthralled. She considered it to be 'sharper and sassier' than the film and desperately wanted to be on stage, singing and dancing as Millie. This was the stuff of her dreams. All those little shows she had 'directed' and performed in as a little girl in Bishop's Waltham, the dance classes, the drama schools, had been leading to this moment. She mustn't fail now. After four days of intensive and stressful rehearsals she auditioned for 12 American backers.

'It was terrifying but it was a personal challenge that I absolutely had to do,' she recalled. Amanda had given it her best shot and thought she had done OK but there followed an agonising wait before she knew one way or another. There was added stress when a tape of her audition, bound for the director Michael Mayer in Vancouver, was blown up at the airport! But, as always, she found the funny side in adversity. When her agent explained that the airport security guards thought it was a 'suspicious package', Amanda shot back, 'Did they watch it then?'

After what seemed like an eternity Amanda finally got the news she had been waiting for: she had landed the part. One of the first people she called to tell was Les Dennis. 'He was thrilled because he has been in the West End himself in *Chicago*,' she said. 'He's still proud of everything I do. And he said to me, "Have no doubts, I will be there on the opening night."'

The run would clash with the filming of a third series of *Cutting It* but a storyline was engineered so that she was able to return for a part of the series that involved Allie setting both of the hairdressing salons on fire before running back to London.

As well as having to learn the Charleston and take tap-dancing and ballet lessons for *Millie*, she worked out three times a week with a personal trainer to help her get into shape and build her stamina. It was a demanding schedule.

Although she was a keen gymnast as a child, she wasn't a trained dancer, and the routines were hard and exhausting. She never did like her feet, which she thought had been made 'all bony' from doing gymnastics. Now she complained that she had 'dancer's feet with manky skin'. She was fitter than she had ever been before and, although toned, she was actually heavier now because of muscle weight.

When launching the show in July 2003 Amanda took the opportunity to point out the differences between Millie and herself. 'I have always known where my heart is and, although sometimes it didn't work out, I never chased after the wrong man. I definitely feel much more ready to take on the responsibility of starring in a West End show. I don't know if I could have done it before.'

When she was asked how she was bearing up at the moment, she replied, 'The last eighteen months have made me a stronger, tougher person. I was strong before but now I'm doubly strong.'

Later Sarah Parish told reporters that Amanda was 'glowing', and they regularly phoned each other and giggled over the various people that the newspapers said she was dating. 'She's having so much fun going out with the girls. She's the happiest she has ever been at the moment,' she said.

There was a secret reason why Amanda was so happy. She had been tentatively seeing a new man.

ELEVEN

CHRIS HUGHES

'I realised that she is funny, generous,
kind and a right laugh, so I just went for it.'
Chris Hughes on Amanda Holden

L ong-haired 30-year-old record-company producer
Chris Hughes drove a £50,000 BMW X5 jeep and
owned a £300,000 flat in Chelsea, west London. He was
the son of Les's agent, Mike Hughes, and had known
Amanda for around 10 years but there was never any
question of a romance – not while she was with Les
anyway. Chris had always fancied Amanda but she had no
idea. He was there to support her when she split with Les
but she was surprised when their relationship as friends
took a different turn.

Chris had taken Amanda out to dinner that January and
the pair felt closer than they ever had before. Concerned
about diving into another relationship, Amanda took
things slowly and was still thinking of him as a good friend

to begin with but her feelings were changing. As they grew ever closer they were keen to keep their relationship under wraps. She needed some breathing space and didn't want yet more press intrusion into her personal life. And Chris was a private man, unused to the celebrity spotlight.

After a series of discreet dinner dates at each other's home they spent a weekend in the Cotswolds, six weeks into their 'new' relationship, and that was when Amanda knew she loved him. 'I didn't want to say goodbye. I knew right then he was "The One" – he made me laugh, he was sexy and ticked every box. I knew I couldn't live without him.'

Amanda was secretly amused by media speculation that she was dating Jamie Theakston when she was actually seeing Chris. 'That was hysterical,' she recalled in interview. 'I'd been seeing my boyfriend for months and had managed to keep it a secret. I remember thinking, I know what's going to happen here. The press think I'm single, they think Jamie's single, they're going to try to put us together.'

Having learned her lesson about public snogging, she was not about to make the same mistake. 'At the end of filming we all went for dinner at the Century Club [a private members' club in Shaftesbury Avenue frequented by media types] and apparently Jamie and I "canoodled". Well, I swear on my life, if I was going to do any canoodling, it would be with my boyfriend in private and not at the Century Club, which is swarming with journalists!'

The romance with Chris took Amanda by surprise because they had barely even been friends – more like acquaintances who had bumped into each other over the years. Besides, he had never been short of glamorous female company. 'I couldn't even say we were friends,' said Amanda. 'We'd only met three times in ten years, at various dos.'

But, just when things were looking cosy, they parted in the May after news of their relationship had been made public. He found the attendant publicity too stressful. Suddenly he was being talked about in the press, they were photographed together and he was overwhelmed by being in the spotlight. Amanda seemed to take their split in a relaxed, mature way, telling the *People*, 'Chris and I are no longer together. The relationship wasn't working out and it's best for both of us to move on. But we will remain good friends.'

However, she was far more upset than she let on. After all she had been through, the glint of some stability in her life with a man she truly loved was a welcome relief – if totally unexpected. Privately, it seems, she knew the power of playing it 'cool' and she didn't want to make matters worse with Chris by coming across as too needy. But she secretly never gave up hope that he would return to her. And she didn't have to wait long.

Chris was missing Amanda and he realised that he wanted her back in his life. So he picked up the phone and called her, and their relationship resumed. He later explained his feelings: 'Before we got together I thought that my life might be too intruded on if I started seeing her because, as a music producer, I'm more used to being behind the scenes – but when I got to know her, I realised that she is funny, generous, kind and a right laugh, so I just went for it.'

For once, Amanda had managed to keep her impulsive instincts in check and learned that there was value in sometimes letting things take their natural course. 'He had to go away and do his own journey. I just waited and I had the strength to do it. I knew if he didn't come back, he wasn't the man for me,' she said. 'Chris found being followed everywhere strange. Now we've been properly together for three months without anyone intruding and we're really happy. I always said I'd tell the press when I did get a boyfriend and now I can say, "Yes, it's Chris Hughes and he's a very handsome man."'

Never one to stay private for too long, a happy-in-love Amanda admitted that she was probably too young when she married Les and should have taken heed of his warnings at the time. But, like many a young woman, she led with her heart and not her head – a trait that has stayed with her. 'With hindsight, I didn't feel as if I'd been living in my own skin for a while. Maybe I did marry too young but I don't regret anything in my life. Les and I had a loving relationship and we were together for ten years. That's not bad in this business.'

Now she was on a high, and felt that all the uncertainty

and pain were in the past. She had coped with everything – including all the flak – and remained unbowed. In a defiant stance she proclaimed, 'I'm a woman, not a girl any more. I'm fearless. I've coped with so much but nothing has broken me and nothing will.'

Even bumping into Neil Morrissey on the showbiz circuit was no longer an issue. The pair met in July at a charity ball at Stowe School, Buckinghamshire, to mark the British Grand Prix. A string of famous faces were invited, including actor Jason Statham and his then model-turned-actress girlfriend Kelly Brook, and there were performances by Craig David and Atomic Kitten. Amanda, wearing an expensive Versace dress, had gone along with her mum and Sarah Parish, and Neil arrived with television producer Tamzin Locise on his arm. Any awkwardness was quickly dispersed as they exchanged greetings and chatted just like old friends.

That summer Amanda and Chris took their first holiday abroad together – to the magnificent Hotel Villa San Michele, perched on the hills above Florence, Italy. Dating from the 15th century, the Villa's façade is attributed to no less than Michelangelo and is considered to be one of the most romantic hotels in the world. For the first few days of their holiday they relaxed at the hotel, enjoying the splendour of the Renaissance building and the stunning views of the city below as they sat around the pool or had a drink on the terrace. Long lunches and siestas were followed by an early-evening stroll through the romantic Italian gardens, bursting with lemon trees and fragrant roses.

Chris had never been to Florence and Amanda, who loved the city, was eager to show him around – but that was until she arrived at the hotel and then felt reluctant to leave! 'I'd been to Florence so many times before that we only went into town about twice and I gave him the fastest whistlestop tour ever,' she later recalled. 'I basically said, "There's the Duomo, there's something else, there's my favourite shop. Now let's go back to the hotel!"'

Although Amanda still had her home in north London, she was spending the majority of her time at the penthouse Chris had just bought by the riverside in Richmond, Surrey. Amanda loved the place and she helped him to celebrate the purchase with a romantic dinner at a nearby Italian restaurant.

By September 2003 she had pretty much moved in full-time. Amanda loved walking along the riverside path, dining out locally and then relaxing back at the apartment. Life with Chris was bliss and they were as excited as two teenagers in love for the first time. 'Chris is so much fun, he is so playful. He's made me remember what being young is all about. That's one of his best qualities – he's always ready to be the silly bugger and mess about. I'm more the grown-up, so it's a good combination.'

But Amanda was worried about starring in *Thoroughly Modern Millie*. It was the first time she had ever taken on a singing-and-dancing role, and the weight and responsibility of 'carrying' the show rested on her shoulders. It was a huge undertaking for her and a big gamble. If she failed to cut it, the knives would be out and her professional reputation would be badly damaged.

The opening night in October 2003 caused a stir both on and off stage. Chris, and Amanda's mum and dad, Judith and Les, were there to support her and the press was out in force, eager to see how she would cope in a major musical. And there were plenty of sceptics waiting for her to fall flat on her face.

Amanda borrowed a beautiful Valentino gown to make a graceful arrival but the image was marred somewhat when, as she later put it, 'My boob fell out!' She was feeling unwell and exhausted but this was probably due to nerves. It was the most daunting night of her life. Even the scenery appeared to have stage fright when it got stuck during the performance, requiring a three-minute break while it was fixed.

In the event, Amanda danced and sang her way through the show with aplomb, and was rewarded with a standing ovation.

'It was a roller coaster, like riding the Big One in Blackpool,' she said. 'I was very nervous at the beginning, as I'm standing alone on the stage but when everyone else came on it was fine. I thoroughly enjoyed every second. It's really been a dream come true.'

As she took her final bow she blew a kiss to Chris in the audience. 'I wanted to show him that I knew he was out there,' she said. 'He was very nervous for me.'

Backstage in her dressing room she had a stream of well-wishers. 'My dressing room looks like a florist,' said a beaming Amanda. 'People I worked with years ago have contacted me to wish me good luck. It's been great. I knew my family and boyfriend were in the audience, and I just performed for them really.'

Amanda later revealed that every night on stage she sang Millie's big number, 'Jimmy', for her beloved granddad, Jimmy, whom she called 'Papa'. He had been diagnosed with Alzheimer's in 2000. 'He had followed my career since I was three, when he would tape my sister and I singing and performing our own shows. He said he would know I had finally made it when he saw my name in lights. Now that had finally happened and every night I sang that song for my Papa, and, despite the Alzheimer's, he knew.'

At the after-show party at the Waldorf Astoria Hotel, proud Chris warmly hugged and kissed Amanda in front of 600 guests.

The following day Amanda and Chris eagerly checked the newspapers for reviews of the show, and Amanda was amused to find that they seemed to be more interested in her 'wardrobe malfunction'. 'It was a disaster because, apart from getting quite good reviews, there were loads of pics of my boob with captions like, "Holden onto her nipple!" You just think, God, you work your arse off for two and a half hours on stage and then your tit upstages you!'

In truth, the reviews were mixed – although most of the criticism was aimed at the production, rather than Amanda,

Amanda Holden with parents Judith and Frank.

© Rex Features

With Les Dennis – Amanda and he
were married in Bournemouth in
June 1995.   © *Rex Features and PA Photos*

Above: Amanda with *The Grimleys* co-stars Craig Kelly, James Bradshaw, Noddy Holder and (front) Brian Conley. © *Rex Features*

Right: Amanda with *Wild at Heart* co-stars Lucy-Jo Hudson, Stephen Tomkinson, Luke Ward-Wilkinson, Rafaella Hutchinson and Hayley Mills. © *Rex Features*

Above: Amanda with Craig Urbani and Mark McGee for *Thoroughly Modern Millie*. *© Getty Images*

Right: Bumping into Neil Morrissey in July 2003 at a British Grand Prix charity bash in Stowe, Bucks.

© Rex Features

Above: The *Cutting It* stars. From left to right, Angela Griffin, Sian Reeves, Amanda, Lucy Gaskell and Sarah Parish.

© *PA Photos*

Below: Amanda and Chris Hughes at a match between his favourite team Everton and Norwich.

© *Rex Features*

Above left: Sharing a laugh on her hen night before her marriage to Chris Hughes with her best pals including (seated) Lucy Jo Hudson, Angela Griffin, Sarah Parish and Sian Reeves.

Above right: Amanda training for the 2008 London Marathon with her Cairn terrier Fudge.

Below: At the Royal Variety Performance in 2007 with Piers Morgan and Simon Cowell.

© Rex Features

Above: On *The Early Show* with Harry Smith in America.

© *Rex Features*

Below: Amanda with her *Britain's Got Talent* co-stars Ant and Dec.

© *Getty Images*

Above: Amanda with daughter Lexi as a baby. © *PA Photos*

Right: *Shrek: The Musical* was to feature, clockwise from top left, Nigel Lindsay as Shrek, Amanda as Princess Fiona, Nigel Harman as Lord Farquaad and Richard Blackwood as Donkey. © *PA Photos*

who was generally considered to have done well. The main criticism was that the new songs that had been added for the show failed to impress and that the production, at 150 minutes long, was overstretched and 'soulless'.

'Amanda Holden is appealing as the girl from the sticks,' said *The Times*, while the *Daily Mail* described her as 'very good, and very personable'. However, the critic for the *Independent* was particularly scathing about the show and attacked everything, including Amanda, whom he condemned as 'bland, so unimpeachable in voice and looks as to seem computer-generated'. And the *Daily Mirror* commented, 'Her American accent is passable and she sings adequately but her somewhat perfunctory voice hardly filled the auditorium. There is nothing wrong with her performance. But there is definitely nothing great about it either.'

Another first for Amanda came the following month when she hosted a TV show called *Greasemania*, a one-hour celebration of the hit musical *Grease*. It featured the likes of Girls Aloud, Westlife, Tony Hadley, the Cheeky Girls and *Pop Idol* runner-up Gareth Gates. 'It's the first time I had ever presented anything, so I was really nervous,' said Amanda. 'I was shaking before I went on stage but it's definitely something I want to do more of.'

Working hard on *Millie* gave Amanda Holden little time to do anything else but, at 32, her thoughts were turning towards starting a family. Although she had talked about it endlessly in the past, she admitted that she had never really meant it.

'I terribly want children but I didn't want to have them with Les,' she confessed. 'That's a horrible, brutal thing to say but, when you think that way, you know it's time to move on [from that relationship]. I'm very broody. Maybe I'll have children – wham bam! – in a couple of years and have about four.' Speaking about her love for Chris Hughes, she said, 'I've never been so happy. My dad said, "You're like a little girl again."'

In stark contrast to Amanda's happiness, there was more misery for Les as he split with Leoni. He had been living in Madrid with her and they had been looking for homes to buy, both there and in London. He had told friends that he was madly in love and wanted to marry her. But instead he had returned home in October after it became clear their relationship had broken down. Les moved into a two-bed rented flat above a restaurant in Highgate, north London. And it was to his first wife, Lynne, that he turned to for support as he poured out his pain. Lynne, who lived nearby in Hampstead with their son Philip, was also a shoulder to cry on during the split with Amanda.

'Les is at absolute rock bottom,' said a friend. 'He can't believe another relationship has crumbled. He's asking why. He really thought they had a future together.' His seven-year marriage to Amanda officially came to an end on 18 November 2003 after a judge granted a 'quickie' divorce. But the reason given for the divorce came as a surprise to many because it was officially due to Les's adultery. In papers presented to the High Court's Family Division, Amanda said her husband had revealed his affair in January 2003 – almost three years after her six-week fling with Morrissey – and that the affair was ongoing.

She confirmed she had moved out of their marital home after learning of his infidelity, adding that the news had made it intolerable to live with him. In turn, Les admitted the accusation in his court papers and stated he had no objection to paying the costs of the proceedings. Neither of the stars attended the hearing.

Later that month, Amanda took part in the Royal Variety Performance, along with her *Millie* colleagues, performing a sequence from the show. The musical was continuing to draw theatregoers, and Amanda was now feeling a lot more confident and relaxed in the lead role. 'Everyone keeps saying to me, "Your voice is the best-kept secret ever." But it's not a surprise to anyone who knows me because I'm always singing. It's such a fluffy, feel-good show that, even if I were in the most miserable of moods, I'd cheer up after the first number. Without sounding like Miss World, the company I'm working with are just the nicest bunch of people ever and I'm having a really good time.

'I am madly happy, both in my personal and professional life. Doing *Thoroughly Modern Millie* in the West End has meant I've fulfilled a childhood ambition and, having someone you love in your life, someone lovely to share it with, makes it all complete. There's nothing else I could want.'

But there was a fly in the ointment: a love-struck fan had been stalking her for six months and was now turning up each night outside the stage door at the Shaftesbury Theatre. The six-foot, shaven-headed psychiatric patient believed that he loved her and that she loved him, and he left her obsessive messages of undying love and made lurid suggestions about meeting her at a hotel.

It was Amanda's appearance on *Parkinson* the previous year that had sparked off his obsessive behaviour. When Amanda told the chat-show host, 'I don't have anyone in my life; it's going to take a very brave man to love me and stay with me,' the deluded fan was convinced her words were a personal invitation to him.

He began leaving messages with her agent and even convinced himself that she had returned his calls. He was reported to police and security staff at the theatre were told to look out for him. Eventually, much to Amanda's relief, he stopped coming and she was not bothered by him again.

There was another visitor to the theatre too: her biological father, Frank. He had arranged a meeting via Amanda's agent to see her before she went on stage in November 2003. They spent half an hour together in her dressing room.

'We had a big hug to start with. I gave her a rose. Then I said, "Christ, I never thought I'd see you down the West

End, big signs up with your name on it. I'm very proud of you,"' he recalls. Frank kept the show programme and a handwritten card on which Amanda wrote her address but he didn't see her for another three years.

Having found her 'soulmate' in life, she was no longer so interested in going out with friends. And, particularly after a hard night on stage, she couldn't wait to get home. 'I'm a girl and I love dressing up but now I'm more into going home after the show to eat fish and chips in my grubby tracksuit than partying and being all glam.'

And Chris received the ultimate accolade from Amanda when he superseded Jack Nicholson as the man of her dreams! When the *Sunday Mirror* asked whom she would most like to be stuck in a lift with, she replied, 'Once upon a time I would have said Jack Nicholson but now I would say my boyfriend Chris. I would lurrrrrve to get stuck in a lift with him. I can think of plenty of things we could do to pass away the time until help arrived.'

Meanwhile, there were rumours that Simon Cowell was keen to have her partake in a celebrity version of his hit singing talent show, *The X Factor*. But Amanda was having nothing to do with it. She told the *Newcastle Chronicle*, 'Absolutely one hundred per cent no way. Simon Cowell can go away – he can come and see *Millie* and he can judge me on that performance but that's the only performance he can judge me on. I definitely wouldn't do one of those programmes – I have enough people scrutinising me without that!'

But she was hoping that *Millie* would be watched by some influential bigwigs from Hollywood. Her LA agent was busy trying to persuade some of them to come over to London to watch her in the show. She still had ambition to crack America but, although she was happy to fly out there to meet producers, she was too settled in the UK to contemplate living in LA. 'It would be fantastic to work in LA but I'm not sure I'd like to live there. And I'm not brave enough to sit and wait out there for it to happen and turn down work in England.'

Looking towards her future, she knew that her days of playing sexy young women were numbered. 'Every blonde actress has her time limit before she fizzles out and has to come back and play mistresses and older women. That'll happen to me. I've got probably about four years and then perhaps I'll go and do some producing. Then, hopefully, I'll come back like Joanna Lumley [playing] someone's glamorous mother.'

The New Year could not have had a better starting block because she felt that she had it all. She laughed that she didn't need to make any New Year resolutions because everything she could wish for was already happening.

Amanda had several press and TV interviews lined up to publicise *Mad About Alice* and was so in love that she happily answered any questions about her private life. 'I've found the love of my life,' she told the *People*. 'He's the man of my dreams. I will definitely say we'll be spending our future together.' And she had started to want that future to include marriage, describing Chris to the *TV Times* as her 'soulmate'.

But, just as 2004 looked perfect for her in every way, she was rushed to hospital.

TWELVE

AGONY AND ECSTASY

'I'd love to marry Chris. I'm waiting expectantly.'

Amanda Holden on her relationship
with Chris Hughes

In February 2004 Amanda took a break from performing in *Millie*, and she and Chris Hughes went on what they imagined would be a romantic holiday in Barcelona and Venice. But it turned into a disaster. While they were in Barcelona Chris had been taken ill with diarrhoea, which had confined him to their hotel for much of their stay. An eagerly looked-forward-to holiday took another turn for the worse when Amanda's mobile phone was stolen while she was out shopping.

By the time they were on their way to Venice, Chris was feeling much better and had got his energy back. But then it was time for Amanda to fall ill. No sooner had they arrived than she keeled over with back pain. A worried Chris took her to hospital but the doctor could not determine the cause of it. With Amanda still in pain, they flew back home but that evening the stabbing sensation got worse. Chris phoned for an ambulance, and she was rushed to hospital and put on an antibiotic drip.

Doctors diagnosed a kidney infection and she was to remain in hospital for four days while being treated. Amanda's understudy stepped into the role of *Millie* in the meantime. To Amanda's relief, the pain gradually subsided and she returned home but was under orders to rest, and it was another few weeks before she returned to the stage on 17 March 2004. That night she received an even more rapturous applause than normal after the show had ended. A smiling Amanda told the audience that she had put on five pounds during her month off. 'I just want to say thank you very much. You were a really smashing audience and made it very easy for me,' she said.

Amanda's illness had kept her away from the Olivier awards on 22 February 2004, where she had been shortlisted for Best Actress for her role as Millie Dillmount. In the event, there was no need for her 'winner's speech' to be read out because the award went to hot favourite Maria Friedman for *Ragtime*.

Millie ended its run on 26 June 2004. It had been a fulfilling and exhilarating show for Amanda but she was pleased to be able to rest and spend some quality time at home with Chris. But she couldn't resist a small role in an episode of *French & Saunders* for a sketch in which

King Lear was performed as if it were an episode of one of Amanda's favourite shows – *Footballers' Wives*. Also appearing in the sketch were Michelle Collins, Denise Van Outen and Brian Cox.

Chris, who loved to give nice surprises to Amanda, excelled himself when, after a year of searching, he managed to track down her dream car – a cream Morris Minor convertible with a red leather interior. After bringing it home he parked it in their garage and told Amanda there was a big package for her there. When Amanda walked in and saw the car, she was overcome with emotion and burst into tears.

Now she had more time to think of personal matters, her mind once more was focused on life with Chris and what the future held for them. And the more she thought about it, the more she realised how much she loved him and wanted them to take that special step further. In an interview with DJ and presenter Lauren Laverne, host of ITV1's *Orange Playlist*, she said that they were getting close to walking down the aisle – even though he hadn't actually proposed.

'I'd love to marry Chris. I'm waiting expectantly. We've reached the point where marriage is the next step. It's the most amazing love I've ever experienced. Having a family is important to me and knowing that Chris will make an amazing dad is a comforting thought.'

A few days later Chris made his move. Ever the one for surprises, he had planned this one for maximum effect.

He invited some friends around for dinner and, during the course of the evening, he visited the bathroom and then called for Amanda. A puzzled Amanda wondered what he wanted and, when she got to the bathroom, she saw Chris standing outside, looking shaken. Worried, she anxiously asked him what the matter was and was taken aback when he told her there was a huge spider in the shower, and could she please capture it.

Although Amanda knew he was frightened of spiders and was used to having to deal with them herself, she did think he was being particularly wimpish to call for her help – particularly in front of guests. But he was insistent and, rather grudgingly, she went off to find a glass and some paper with which to capture the spider. Amanda shared the joke with her invited guests that she was having to capture a spider because Chris couldn't do it himself and then returned to the bathroom, where Chris was still waiting like a frightened schoolgirl.

She couldn't help but smile at how helpless he looked and asked him to point to where the scary creature was lurking. Chris gingerly opened the door and indicated the shower. Amanda strolled confidently over and pulled back the door to the shower unit, and let out a scream that could be heard throughout the house! But this was no ugly great hairy spider. It was a dazzling diamond engagement ring. A wide-eyed Amanda turned towards Chris, who was smiling broadly. Laughing, he explained, 'Well, I can never surprise you and I knew you wouldn't expect this.'

Chris then proposed and Amanda, shedding tears of joy, managed to blub out, 'Yes.' They hugged and kissed before returning to the dinner table to share the news with their delighted guests, and toasted the occasion with champagne.

Amanda excitedly told all her family and friends about her wonderful news, and wasted no time in planning the event and in choosing her wedding dress and the ring she wanted.

A few days later a radiant Amanda got the chance to show off her £20,000 engagement ring when she was one of the main presenters at the British International Film Awards at the Hammersmith Palais that November. And she was happy to talk to the throng of reporters about the proposal. 'Chris said he wanted me to have such a big ring so that any man would see from about a mile down the road that I was off the market.' She added, 'He's extraordinarily funny and very good looking – well, I think so anyway.'

Ever one to try new things, she also said that she was hoping to break into the pop industry – with the help of her record producer fiancé, Chris. Amanda was keen to launch herself as a singer and to be able to do her own TV specials. 'I'd absolutely love to start a career in music and it's something we've discussed,' she said. 'I'm a bit old to be the new Rachel Stevens and too young to be Dolly Parton. I see myself somewhere in between.'

Meanwhile, there were ups and downs on the acting front. The one-off feature-length TV comedy drama *Ready When You Are, Mr McGill* had gone out on Sky Movies in September to high acclaim. The film, written by award-winning writer Jack Rosenthal, was also shown on ITV1 the following Christmas. But it was the end of the line for Amanda's lukewarm sitcom, *Mad About Alice*, when it was announced that there would be no further series. By this stage Amanda finally admitted it was not up to scratch though, as she said to the *Sun*, 'The show had ratings over five million.'

She still had many other ambitions to fulfil. Among them, she longed to appear in a period drama and often joked that she would love to make a film on Holkham Beach near her home in Norfolk – a 'bonnet drama' – in which she ran along her favourite beach towards her lover while someone splashed the waves against her petticoats. That particular scenario had yet to happen but she did get a taste of doing a period drama when she had a role in *Agatha Christie's Marple: 4.50 From Paddington*, alongside Geraldine McEwan as the famous sleuth and a star cast that included John Hannah, Niamh Cusack, David Warner, Rob Brydon, Pam Ferris and her *Cutting It* co-star Ben Daniels.

Amanda played Miss Marple's friend Lucy Eyelesbarrow in the ITV1 drama, who goes undercover for her as a housekeeper at Rutherford Hall to hunt for the body of a murdered woman believed to have been buried in the grounds. The opportunity to wear 1950-style corsets and dresses was as much an attraction of the role as anything else.

'The chance to wear gorgeous frocks and wonderful hairstyles really appealed. I admit it. I'm so shallow!' she recalled in interview. 'It's a brilliant chance for me to be worlds away from the kind of role that I normally get offered. Hopefully, I'll get a couple of bonnet dramas out of this. I never tire of going into a make-up van because you arrive looking absolutely dreadful and leave looking like a million dollars.'

In another effort to widen her acting scope she was scheduled to play a psychotic stalker in a two-part ITV thriller *The Kindness of Strangers*. But in the event, she was offered the chance to work in South Africa. Instead, Hermione Norris took over her role while Amanda looked forward to starring in a big new six-part ITV series called *Wild at Heart*.

Amanda and co-star Stephen Tompkinson would play husband and wife who run a game reserve in South Africa, with filming to start in May of the next year. With such a big undertaking coming up, requiring spending four months in South Africa, Amanda and Chris decided not to rush their wedding because they wanted plenty of time to plan it, so they decided on December 2005.

But her professional and personal plans were disrupted when she discovered she was pregnant.

Amanda had flown out to South Africa to start filming *Wild at Heart* in May 2005. But one week into filming she was feeling sick and tired. She was in a different country with local food and a demanding schedule but, nevertheless, she began to wonder. When a pregnancy test proved positive, she was shocked. 'We didn't think it would happen quite so fast. It was literally the first week we were over there I found out,' she was later to say. 'The only person I told was Chris.'

Never one to refuse a glass of wine or champagne, she managed to pull the wool over the collective eyes of cast and crew when she stopped drinking alcohol. 'I told everyone I was hugely professional and I never drank while I was working. They believed me, which was astounding!'

The long days, heat and terrain made it tough and uncomfortable. Knowing she was pregnant made her feel different: more vulnerable, cautious and protective of what she was carrying. But it was early days and she was determined not to tell anyone about her pregnancy until a later stage. 'It was hard. I was completely knackered but I had to keep it a secret. No one on set knew to begin with but people started to get suspicious.'

After a couple of months' filming, her increasing chest size had been noticed. 'The director came up to me and said, "The editor says it's all going very well and he made a joke about how your boobs look huge in one scene and not in the other." They didn't put two and two together though.'

Physically it was demanding. In one scene her character's daughter, Olivia, is bitten by a snake and Amanda has to rush her home, driving over bumpy ground in a Land

Rover. After one take Amanda was worried about all the jolting but didn't know how to express her concern without giving the game away. Eventually, she hit upon the idea of pretending that she had a bad back, so that they gave her some cushions, and she put them all around her midriff, including around and under her tummy, to give her protection and support.

The stunning landscape and exotic animals were already losing their appeal and she later admitted that she often wanted to be back home in England amid the concrete and skyscrapers, rather than out in the wilds near Johannesburg.

After nine weeks into filming Amanda returned to England for a break and had a couple of scans. Then around the 12th week of her pregnancy she told everyone, and felt much more relieved and relaxed when she returned to work in South Africa. 'Once I could tell people, everyone was so sweet and considerate. As the baby started getting bigger, the weather got hotter. So I was followed everywhere by a man with an umbrella and a footstool. I wouldn't get that sort of treatment at home!'

And her co-star Stephen Tompkinson, father to a four-year-old daughter named Daisy, was full of advice. 'He was brilliant at being honest and telling me quite graphically all about his wife's birthing pool, and about how her breasts leaked at a wedding when another baby cried!'

That September, having finished filming in South Africa, Amanda and Chris relaxed on the luxurious

Necker Island in the Caribbean, owned by tycoon Sir Richard Branson. It was to be one of her best holidays ever. 'The island is stunning. There were twelve of us and the staff were so accommodating. We dined on the beach and on cliff tops – you could probably eat on the roof if you wanted to. If you were hungry in the middle of the night, you could help yourself to something in the kitchen. It was like being in a gorgeous open house. We could also do any watersports we wanted. Richard Branson was there. He is the most fantastic host – always organising things and just great fun.'

With the baby due in January, the couple decided to put their wedding off further until after the birth. In an interview with the *Daily Mirror* she inadvertently let slip that she was expecting a girl. Talking about their wedding date, she remarked, 'We are engaged but we have not got a date. He [Chris] is fantastic. He is talking to her and massaging the bottom of my back.'

To her delight, Amanda's good friend Jane Wall, who had played PC Di Worrell in *The Bill*, also fell pregnant around the same time. At a movie premiere in London for the 'chick flick' movie *In Her Shoes*, starring Cameron Diaz and Shirley MacLaine, Amanda and Jane laughingly compared their growing bumps.

Both had very different views when it came to giving birth. 'I'm going to have every drug available but Jane's going to be all nice and natural,' she said. 'None of that hippy rubbish like a water birth for me – just drugs! Before

I was pregnant I thought I was quite a holistic person. I thought, Yes, I'll have a water birth and I'll do that hypnosis thing where you don't believe in pain. Now I'm pregnant, I'm like, no! I don't want to be brave. I want to be on a bed with a big needle in my back. I don't want to feel anything.'

But Amanda *was* into music therapy – although she was disappointed in her unborn baby's choice! 'I talk to her sometimes but I feel a bit stupid,' she said. 'I also play classical music to her most days – Bach, Beethoven – to make her more intelligent. My own favourite is Abba but I played it for her and I got indigestion, so she's obviously not a fan.'

Amanda was so obsessed with Abba that she wanted to live – and die – by them. Not only had she dumped her boyfriend John Banister with the advice to listen to Abba's 'Winner Takes It All', but she also wanted Abba music to play as she was buried! 'It's in my will for "Dancing Queen" to be played at my funeral as I'm lowered into the ground,' she once remarked.

She had also boldly stated that mums-to-be should 'always wear heels and try to look as glam as possible. Pregnancy is not an excuse.'

As for the wedding, it looked as if they were going to have more than enough time to plan it, as the big day was pushed back even further because they wanted their daughter to be a bridesmaid.

'Having a baby is the biggest commitment you can make to somebody, so we're going to take our time with the wedding,' she said. 'It will probably be a couple of years. I'd love a nice, intimate, small wedding, not a big lavish do. Hopefully, nobody will even know about it until after we've tied the knot.'

Amanda, who often joked about being flat chested, was enjoying the side benefits that pregnancy gave to her curves. 'I would like to keep my new boobs after the baby's born, as I really do love them,' she said.

Impending motherhood made her think about what a wonderful job Judith had made of it with her and Debbie. She was beginning to appreciate the sacrifices, commitment and lack of selfishness required. And she was also beginning to feel guilty. 'Motherhood is a life-changing thing,' she said in interview. 'There will be somebody in your life that will be completely reliant on you. I keep thinking about all those times I rowed with my parents. I just know it's going to happen to me. At some stage my child will turn round and say, "I hate you!" I'm thinking ahead and remembering all the grief I gave my mother.'

In the meantime, she was pleased to be having a relatively easy pregnancy with no mood swings and not even a hint of morning sickness. An initial craving for a white crusty bap with thick butter and cheese soon passed, and then she couldn't stop smelling citrus-flavoured soaps and drinking fizzy water with lime. And, despite worrying that she would find it too hard to give up alcohol, she was relieved to find that she no longer fancied it – apart from an odd glass of champagne and a Guinness.

Amanda and Chris had a restful and happy Christmas at their home in Norfolk as they looked forward to parenthood in the New Year. But the baby's arrival was to take her by surprise.

THIRTEEN

MUM'S THE WORD

'I love being a mum. It sorts all your priorities out.'
AMANDA HOLDEN ON MOTHERHOOD

The New Year was a real life-changing one as Amanda gave birth to her daughter on 21 January 2006, just a month short of her 35th birthday. The baby, Alexa Louise Florence Hughes – known as Lexi – weighed six pounds and was delivered by Caesarean section because Amanda had a low-lying placenta that blocked the birth canal. The suddenness took them by surprise. They had been getting ready to go to the cinema when Amanda suddenly felt that it wasn't such a good idea after all. Instead, they headed for the hospital.

Amanda had hoped to play a CD of her beloved Abba while in labour but, when she opened the case, it was empty. Some nurses came to the rescue – not with a replacement Abba album, but a free CD given away with a newspaper. 'It was Burt Bacharach, who I love, so it was even more kitsch!' she later said with a laugh.

When told she would need a Caesarean, she was apprehensive because a few people had told her how 'awful' it was. But the birth went very smoothly. 'My friend, who had a baby naturally ten days after me, couldn't sit down for ages. But I didn't think it was a big deal,' Amanda said afterwards. 'I was desperate for her to be an Aquarian like me but she was born half an hour too early. I'm a believer in fate, so that was meant to be.'

The niece of a friend of Amanda's was called Lexi and Amanda had always liked the name but she and Chris decided on Alexa in case she wanted a more 'mature' name when she got older. Louise is Amanda's middle name and Florence her grandmother's middle name, and Amanda's favourite city.

After five days in hospital Amanda returned home. She was surprised at how active she was. Just four nights after leaving hospital she and Chris went out for a curry.

Although she had talked of having children for years, she was never confident that she would take well to being a mother. So it came as a nice surprise to see that she shone in this most important and taxing role. 'When I had Lexi in hospital, I was bathing her and the nurses asked if I'd been around children before. I was like, "No,"' she later explained. 'I said to Chris that I thought I was playing the part of being a mum and then I really got into it. I think babies can sense if you're nervous or not that confident, so

I just went for it. You know you're not going to drop your baby, you know you're not going to drown your baby, so you just think logically and sensibly about it.'

She described being a mum as the happiest experience of her life. Her career had always been uppermost in her thoughts but now she had another priority in life and she couldn't have been happier. Despite the pressure that many mothers feel to breastfeed, Amanda was upfront about her decision not to. She said it was what she wanted to do and that there was no reason why she would not bond with the child as a result. Amanda, who was eight stone before falling pregnant, gained only a stone and a half during pregnancy and she returned to eight stone, four pounds in super-quick time – without dieting. She was a healthy vegetarian and said she stuck to adding only 200 calories a day to her diet. 'But I never deprived myself of anything. If I wanted a Danish pastry, I'd have it. I love my food but I was really aware of what I was putting into my body because I had a little life inside me.'

After she came out of hospital she had only half a stone to lose. She couldn't go to the gym because of her Caesarean but she walked the dogs every day and the weight just fell off. Later, to tone up, she had a personal trainer who took her through some gentle stomach crunches and she said that carrying Lexi around had given her arms a great work out.

Just three weeks after giving birth Amanda attended London Fashion Week in hot pants! 'My mum told me she was in hot pants two weeks after having me,' she explained. 'So when she bought me some from Top Shop, I squeezed into them for London Fashion Week.'

Before the birth Amanda had felt the urge to have a go at writing children's stories and wrote some involving her Cairn terrier dogs, Nobby and Fudge, which she planned to read to her daughter when she got older. 'They all have a moral because I'm old fashioned and I like children to learn a little bit,' she said. 'The morals include making sure your parents are always in sight, don't get lost, don't run away, and what is good and what bad to eat.'

Amanda followed the rule of maternity nurse Gina Ford's best-selling guide *The Contented Little Baby Book* when it came to bringing up Lexi. Dubbed the 'Queen of Routine', Ford advocates a strictly regimented method for raising infants with feeds and sleeps all taking place at the same time every day. From when she was just a few months old Lexi was in bed by 7pm, Amanda would wake her at 7am and she had a 2-hour nap at 1pm. 'We lived our life around her.'

The routine enabled Amanda and Chris to have some time to themselves instead of being constantly at Lexi's beck and call. She had been weaned on to solids by the time she was five months old and her regular sleeping pattern meant that Amanda could catch up on everything and also have time to 'chill out on the sofa and read'.

Three days after Amanda gave birth *Wild at Heart* had gone out on ITV1. The critics may not have liked it but the public did. The opening episode set the scene for the rest of the series as Bristolian vet Danny Trevanion (Stephen Tompkinson) takes care of a poorly monkey, which had been locked in a basement. His wife, Sarah (Amanda), is adamant they must rehabilitate it into the wilds of South Africa. She suggests that the adventure will bring the family closer together.

So off they go with their three kids in tow. However, Leopard's Den, the wildlife centre they come to, is in a state of disrepair but that problem is soon resolved when the family decide to stay out there and turn it into a first-class game reserve. The story was more than a little contrived and twee and, of course, the critics attacked it with the all the subtlety of a bunch of hyenas.

'It's hard to quantify just how much tosh this all is,' thundered *The Times*; '. . . a creaky start to the series,' said the *Sunday Times*; the *Daily Star* dismissed it as 'stupid and annoying'. But it proved to be hugely popular with viewers, who considered the uncomplicated, heart-warming story to be the perfect Sunday night treat – a look-good/feel-good experience, combining family drama with magnificent African animals in a breathtaking landscape.

The opening episode was watched by a whopping 9.9 million. Later in the run it reached nearly 11 million and was in the top-10 highest-rated shows of 2006. Not surprisingly, a second series was quickly commissioned.

The BAFTAs in May provided another chance for Amanda to glam herself up and go out for the night, and she attracted enviable stares in a slinky backless green Ashley Isham dress.

The following month she flew out to South Africa with her mum, Chris and Lexi for a second series of *Wild at Heart*. Chris later returned to England but frequently visited his family.

'I couldn't leave Lexi behind – that would be dreadful,' she said. 'Chris couldn't bear to be away from either of us – or, at least, I like to think it wasn't just the baby!'

But leaving Lexi while she was filming was emotionally tough for the new mum. 'She was always surrounded by people cuddling her but I did feel guilty even though I knew I could see her during my lunch break,' she said. 'I also took her to see the lions in their enclosure and took photos of the animals for her baby book.'

Amanda's character, Sarah, had been spiced up for the second series. 'She was too nice,' Amanda later explained. 'It's very tough playing a nice person after some of the characters I've played, such as Mia in *Cutting It*. It's so much better being a bitch! Sarah's really career-minded and feisty in the new series and out in a Jeep instead of inside baking cakes. It's a hundred per cent different and, in my opinion, even better than the last series. It's much more of a challenge.'

It was also Amanda who suggested that Hayley Mills play the role of her mum, Caroline, who was to join them in South Africa. She had seen her on a Eurostar train to Paris when it suddenly struck her that she would be perfect to play Sarah's mum. So she contacted one of the executive producers and Hayley was signed up.

Meanwhile, Les Dennis had found new love. Having been down in the dumps after splitting from Leoni, Les, now 52, had fallen for yet another younger woman – life coach Claire Nicholson, who was 18 years his junior. They had first met the previous November at the fundraising Butterfly Ball, in memory of former *Holby City* actress Laura Sadler, who fell to her death from a balcony.

He was charmed when she cheekily asked him for a dance and a romance had slowly developed. They had a series of dinner dates and visited each other's house with increasing frequency. The following Valentine's Day he bought her a huge bouquet.

Les was feeling happier than he had been in years. Where *Celebrity Big Brother* had not been at all what he might have hoped for, his decision to play himself in an episode of Ricky Gervais's new comedy series *Extras* proved to be a masterstroke. The storyline saw him taking the mickey out of his downbeat self and, in doing so, Les went some way to exorcising the ghosts of his past. He had shown the public that he was able to laugh at himself.

In the episode, Gervais, who played film extra Andy, gets a role in Les's pantomime, *Aladdin*. Les introduces Andy to his much younger girlfriend Simone but he is on the verge of a breakdown due to the many setbacks in his career. After discovering that Simone has been cheating on him with a stagehand, he cracks up in the middle of the pantomime and starts venting his anger at the children in the audience.

Les knew that doing *Extras* was a risk when he read the script and was aware that it could just be, as he saw it, 'a piss-take' but he thought it was the chance to change people's perception of him and get rid of the 'sad Les' label. In the event, viewers and critics loved it, and he was widely praised for his performance.

After six months of filming in South Africa Amanda was happy to spend her time just being a stay-at-home mum for a while. 'I love being a mum. It sorts all your priorities out. I still want to work but, unless I can have Lexi with me, I'm not interested,' she said in interview.

Motherhood had made her more sensitive and emotional, and she found she easily broke into tears. 'There was a time when I could watch the news and it wouldn't affect me that much but now it reduces me to tears,' she said. 'I'm thinking, What a horrible world my child's going to be growing up in! You become very protective when you're a parent but, at the same time, more vulnerable.'

She had sent Frank some photographs of Lexi and told him all about her but he wrote asking if he could meet the baby in person. The last time he had seen Amanda was three years earlier when she was starring on the West End stage in *Thoroughly Modern Millie*. Amanda was determined to bring as much love into her own family as she could. Now she was happy and fulfilled with Chris and Lexi she could develop her relationship with Frank. They met again over coffee at a hotel in Cornwall, near the home he shared with his partner Pauline in Torpoint. Chris was also there – the first time the two men had met.

'She'd come down to see her mother and I said I'd like to meet up,' Frank said in interview. 'Lexi sat with me and I thought, Wow, this is great. As soon as you get a baby in your arms, you've got that bond. Chris was very pleasant and shook my hand.'

Amanda later remarked, 'We're friends now and I've introduced him [Frank] to Lexi. I just thought it was the grown-up thing to do.'

By the time she was one year old Lexi was sleeping for 12 hours at night. Gina Ford's routine had been challenging but was paying dividends.

Amanda also took a leaf out of Katie Price's book when it came to balancing motherhood with her own wants in life. She felt it was important for mothers to find some time to be able to treat themselves every now and then. Chris would babysit for her when she went to a beauty session. To her amazement, Amanda said that, far from losing her figure, it even improved after the birth. 'My tummy always had a bit of a paunch but it has actually got flatter since I've had a baby.' However, she said that she wouldn't shy away from having cosmetic surgery at any time in the future, once things started to sag. 'If I ever felt upset that everything was falling and I knew I could do something about it, I'd have a facelift. I just love makeover programmes. It can't change you if you're unhappy inside but, otherwise, why not?'

After a turbulent few years in her personal life Amanda had become philosophical about how she felt her life was back in a good place again, believing in a form of karma – that how you get treated depends on how you treat others.

But, like any working mum, she was constantly tired. Always obsessively tidy and house proud, Amanda had to come to terms with the fact that the house could not always look like a show home. 'I'm knackered most of the time! I've also started letting things go – not making the bed – and that's a big deal!'

Now weighing eight stone, four pounds, she was slightly heavier than she was before her pregnancy but felt it was now the ideal weight for her, as she did not want to look too gaunt. She felt it was good to carry a bit of weight in her face as she got older and joked that 'it saved on Botox!'

The second series of *Wild at Heart* began on Sunday, 14 January 2007, and such was its continuing appeal that Amanda was contracted to make a third series.

Meanwhile, plans for Amanda and Chris's delayed wedding were taking a more concrete shape. Chris recalled going to a wedding when he was three and so he wanted Lexi to be around that age, so that she could be a bridesmaid and actually be able to remember it later.

They set the wedding date for December 2008 and it was to be held at the exclusive private members' club and hotel, Babington House, set in 18 acres of Somerset country parkland. There was a chapel in the grounds where the ceremony would take place, followed by a reception in the main house. Chris's best man would be his closest friend and one of his oldest, Formula 1 driver David Coulthard.

Amanda had always loved the month of December and the anticipation of Christmas, so that was why she chose the festive period.

Before Lexi had come along she had wanted a wedding with no children. But now she was a mother she wanted lots of children there and planned to provide them with a little party of their own. 'Anyone with kids, dogs or anything can come! I'm hoping it will encourage more of my girlfriends to start having babies,' she said.

But motherhood and the prospect of married life had not caused her to lose her professional ambition. And she still hankered after that elusive break in America. 'I want to be an English "Desperate Housewife" out there,' she stated. 'I've had lots of near misses but I hate giving up and I feel like I have unfinished business.'

But her career was about to take a completely unexpected path that would lead her to even greater fame in a new show that was set to become one of the biggest in the country.

FOURTEEN

BRITAIN'S GOT AMANDA

'I'm the filling in a cynical sandwich.'

AMANDA HOLDEN ON HER PART IN
BRITAIN'S GOT TALENT

Simon Cowell had turned the talent show *The X Factor* into the biggest sensation on British TV, pulling in huge audiences. He had always eyed Amanda as one of his judges and had fancied her way back in 2002 when he was a judge on *Pop Idol*. Now he had her in his sights again for his next big show, *Britain's Got Talent* – a version of his hit US TV show.

Amanda loved the idea of diverse acts being given a showcase for their talent (or lack of it). Old-style variety had disappeared from British TV and so had talent shows such as *Opportunity Knocks* and *New Faces*. Here was a modern new twist.

When Cowell approached her and asked her to be a judge, she had no hesitation in accepting and signed up in

February 2007. 'Pretty much everything he touches turns to gold, so I was delighted to be asked,' she said. Her fellow judges were to be Simon himself and Amanda's former nemesis, Piers Morgan, who was editor of the *Daily Mirror* when it broke the story of her affair with Neil Morrissey. Amanda felt sure she would dislike Morgan and prepared to give him an earful for all the less than flattering remarks his paper had made about her over the years. The show's hosts were popular double act Anthony McPartlin and Declan Donnelly, better known as Ant and Dec.

A master of publicity and enemy of understatement, Cowell told the *Daily Mirror*, 'I've done a lot of audition shows but I've never seen anything like this. It's like *The X Factor* on steroids – it's going to be huge.'

And, ever one to maximise his earnings, the music supremo had been impressed with Amanda's voice in *Thoroughly Modern Millie* and planned big things for her. 'She is a terrific singer in the Doris Day mould,' he said. 'We could have a huge hit with an album with her. I plan to get her to sign up soon.'

Auditions for *BGT* took place in Birmingham, Manchester, Cardiff and London. Among mainstream singers and dancers were off-the-wall acts, such as a rapping granny, a dancing horse and a piano-playing pig!

'The show displays a very eccentric side to Britain, which I love,' raved Simon. But the judges did think some of the acts were a little extreme – such as a transvestite who carried out a midget in a suitcase, who then acted as her horse!

Amanda's particular favourite was Damon Wise, 27. When he came on stage, Amanda asked him what he did and he replied that he was a 'unique speciality act'. Simon, who had been dubbed 'Mr Nasty' by the press for his bluntness towards the acts, grumpily remarked, 'Let's get on with it then.' Backstage, even Ant and Dec were appalled by his lack of manners. 'He's so rude, isn't he?' said Ant.

As Damon opened a trunk and Michael Jackson's 'Earth Song' played, the judges looked intrigued. When he closed the lid there, was a puppet monkey on his arm with a red veil over its head who started miming and jiggling to the song. The sheer absurdity of it had Simon, Piers and Amanda in hysterics – particularly when Bubbles the monkey whipped off the veil, turned and wriggled his bottom at the audience! At the end of the act the audience was on its feet and a chuckling Dec remarked, 'A miming monkey has got a standing ovation. Only in Britain!'

Amanda also loved 29-year-old Victoria Armstrong. Dressed in a red glittery catsuit, she literally caused sparks to fly when she placed a grinding machine against her metal codpiece and breastplate! Amanda told her, 'For me, you don't have to do anything. I'm putting you through just for looking like that. You are one sexy mama.'

Baton twirler Craig Womersley, 17, had the judges admiring his bravery and determination to succeed in doing something that he loved, despite what anybody thought of him. His grandmother had run a majorette troupe and he started idly twirling batons, becoming increasingly competent and enthusiastic. His parents, he said, had tried to stop him from doing it in case he was bullied at school. But, although he realised they were just being kind towards him, he secretly continued and then entered *BGT*.

Craig also received a standing ovation for his performance and afterwards Amanda told him, 'I was really lucky: when I had a dream, my parents were a hundred per cent behind me and always have been. When you have a dream, nobody should stop you. I wanted you to be good and you were fantastic.'

Amanda was often teary-eyed, such as when six-year-old, gap-toothed Connie Talbot sweetly sang 'Somewhere Over the Rainbow'. It reminded her of Lexi, whom she hadn't see for three days, and made her feel that she was a terrible mum for not being with her.

But it wasn't just children who made her emotional. Paul Potts, a 36-year-old former mobile-phone sales manager from Port Talbot, South Wales, said that he had been picked on all his life for his weight and appearance but that he became a different person when he sang. However, he was an unlikely contender for stardom. 'When he shuffled on in his crumpled suit and announced he was often compared to Pavarotti, I had my doubts,' Amanda recalls. 'But when he sang "Nessun Dorma" [from Puccini's *Turandot*] the hairs on my arms stood up and I started to weep.' Overcome with emotion, Amanda announced that she was putting him through to the finals for the man she called 'Papa'.

Amanda was still coming to terms with the death of 'Papa', her granddad Jimmy, who had died just a few days earlier. She later explained, 'My granddad was Welsh and introduced me to classical music. He loved choirs and opera, so I knew I'd go [cry] when Paul sang. The funeral was on Tuesday, so it was all quite fresh. My nan said Papa would have been proud and would have absolutely voted for Paul – she was glad I'd mentioned him.'

Among the eventual finalists who battled it out for glory in 2007 were Paul Potts, Connie Talbot, cocktail-juggling duo the Bar Wizards, Damon Scott, 12-year-old singer Bessie Cursons and street dancers the Kombat Breakers. To Amanda's delight, Paul Potts was crowned the winner, walking away with a £100,000 prize and a slot in that year's Royal Variety Performance. 'I've been in this business for fifteen years,' she said, 'but now I've recognised it's the people you least expect anything of who usually come up trumps. As we say in the business, it's not all teeth and tits!'

BGT had been a sensation, as Simon had promised, regularly pulling in audiences of more than 9 million. It got everyone talking about whom they liked and disliked, and the chemistry between the three bickering judges helped to give the show even more bite. Amanda thoroughly enjoyed being a part of it and looked forward to going to work every day. In fact, she didn't even consider it 'work'. She confided that she would do it for nothing. And she loved the banter with her co-judges, both on and off the screen. To her surprise, she was becoming good friends with Piers Morgan and enjoyed his mischievous humour.

'I spent years cursing him when he was an editor, for lots of horrible stories he published about me, but I'm embarrassed to say I like him. Piers is a real gentleman, cunning, always knows what he's talking about and is very measured in what he says. You can always count on him for a sound bite.'

When she demanded that he apologise for comments made in the *Daily Mirror* about her, he replied, 'Actually, you should be thanking me. You wouldn't be with your handsome music-producer husband and have your lovely daughter today if it hadn't been for my intervention.'

Amanda and Piers often formed an alliance against Simon on the show and enjoyed winding him up by voting through acts that he didn't like. They had even nicknamed him the 'Child Catcher' after the evil panto-like villain in *Chitty Chitty Bang Bang*.

'He's brilliant fun, a great laugh, but he isn't interested in children or domestic issues,' Amanda stated. 'He finds that really boring. I would not bring my daughter to work. I had a photo of her on my phone and Simon just said, "You've got dogs too, haven't you? Have you got a picture of a dog?"'

Amused that flirtatious Simon thought her pretty, Amanda saw the opportunity to score points off him.

'I trust Simon's opinions but he wouldn't get anywhere flirting with me,' she said, laughing. 'He's only four foot! He wouldn't dream of being seriously flirty. Have you seen his built-up shoes?'

The pair clashed during auditions in London when Simon kept leaning over and pressing her eliminating buzzer, much to her irritation, and later she gave him a telling-off. But it was no more than a spat and all part of the teasing game.

The after-show fun started in earnest once 'boss' Simon retired to his bed early. That left Amanda, Piers, and Ant and Dec to carry on drinking at their hotel bar.

But, much as she enjoyed *BGT*, she missed being with Lexi and she was sure that Simon, in mischievous mode, played on her emotions. She told the *News of the World*, 'I miss her like mad when I'm away. Simon knows that, so, when we have to eliminate a child from the show, he always makes me do it. He has a weird sense of humour like that. I think he's trying to toughen me up!'

Sitting between competitive Simon and Piers made her sometimes feel like a mother having to control two naughty schoolboys. 'I'm the filling in a cynical sandwich. They're the naughty boys who pretend they don't care – but, actually, they're both big softies.'

The 'boys' often tried to wind her up whenever they disagreed with her views, sometimes asking, 'What do you know?' But Amanda, who had never been a wilting wallflower, could always shut them up by turning the tables and replying, 'I've been in this business for fifteen years. I've auditioned, performed and acted. What do *you* know?'

While Piers joked that Simon acted like the Pope when he arrived for the show, waving to the crowds, Amanda was impressed by the time he spent with the public. He was never in a hurry to get inside and happily shook hands, cuddled and signed autographs. 'He's very down to earth because he remembers who put him where he is,' she observed.

In May 2007 Amanda announced that she was quitting *Wild at Heart*. She would bow out during the third series, which began filming in June. What had once been an exciting adventure had lost its allure. Now she was a mum to toddler Lexi and she thought it too unsettling to continue to take her out to South Africa for six months of the year.

Also, she had enjoyed the *BGT* experience so much that, to her surprise, she wasn't much interested in acting for the moment. When Simon mentioned how much easier it was just to turn up and be spontaneous, rather than learning lines and acting, she had to agree. Also, *BGT* had put her on a higher level of stardom and Simon Cowell was a generous boss when it came to paying his co-judges' salaries. No wonder she had joked, 'They can no longer afford me on *Wild at Heart*.'

Typical of her penchant for black humour, she knew how she wanted her character to be written out of the show. 'I want to be killed and eaten by a lion. That would be my dream exit!'

BGT was fast becoming the most enjoyable show Amanda had ever worked on. She felt the bad times were well and truly over. Now happily settled in a relationship with a young daughter, she knew that no one was much interested in her private life any more. And all she had been through had helped her cope with anything that was thrown at her. 'In order to get through all that was happening in my private life, I developed a tougher skin,' she said. 'And that was good. Before, I think I had been slightly too sensitive.' The break-up and fallout with Les was a painful time but she sought to find the positives in her life, rather than negatives.

As a young man Chris Hughes had travelled around the world with his best friend, racing driver David Coulthard, and Amanda felt that, if she had met Chris years earlier – instead of Les – he wouldn't have been ready to settle down and they might have drifted apart.

'I wouldn't change my life and I don't think there's any point in regretting the past. Of course you regret the people you might have hurt and upset by what you've said and done but you can't change anything.'

In stark contrast to Les, Chris helped her to see the lighter side of life whenever she was worried, down or concerned. And he also made her laugh. Amanda thought that their relationship was helped by the fact that they were friends for a long time before any romance developed. And having a baby brought them even closer together – although she admitted to being terrified that it might have the opposite effect. 'I believe that having a baby can make or break a relationship and, in our case, it's made us.'

A few days after the *BGT* final in June 2007, a rather reluctant Amanda flew out to South Africa to film her final series. 'This is my last *Wild at Heart*,' she said. 'Then, hopefully, I can just be a judge for the rest of my life.'

FIFTEEN

RIDING THE WAVE

'I want to be doing this show when I'm 90.'
AMANDA HOLDEN ON HER ROLE IN *BRITAIN'S GOT TALENT*

Amanda didn't get her way with having her character Sarah eaten by a lion in her final episode of *Wild at Heart*. But she did get her death wish as flames engulfed the Leopard's Den ranch in a bush fire and Sarah, unable to find her way out through the smoke, never made it out alive. Amanda was pleased that Sarah was killed off because it meant that she couldn't be tempted to return.

Walking away from a successful series is not a step to be taken lightly but Amanda didn't regret it for a moment. She even admitted that she was bored during the six-month-long shoot and couldn't wait to get home. She felt very far from civilisation and she wanted to be with her family. Lexi, who was two in February, had been a babe in arms when Amanda had first taken her to South Africa but now she was proving more of a handful. 'She's inherited the noisy gene from her mother and she's not really quiet on set, so we both got told off a lot,' said Amanda.

Little Lexi was the darling of the cast and she had no shortage of attention. But Amanda felt herself fretting that she couldn't be with her enough when she was working. During breaks in filming Amanda let Lexi stroke giraffes and play with tiger cubs while she took lots of pictures and videos to show Daddy back home. But Chris was later alarmed at quite how close Lexi had been allowed to get to the wild animals.

Filming Sarah's death scenes was the most exciting thing Amanda had done throughout the series because there was a lot of action and she did as many of the stunts as they would allow her to do. 'I felt like Angelina Jolie in *Tomb Raider*,' she said. 'There was genuine danger. There was loads of gas, smoke and fire. It was a hot day as well and it was all very scary.'

But, as usual, Amanda couldn't help but turn the most fraught moments into a joke. And as the smoke filled the house, reminiscent of the dry ice used for the lookalike, soundalike talent show *Stars in Their Eyes*, Amanda jumped out and said the show's catchphrase: 'Tonight, Matthew, I'm going to be . . .'

Former *EastEnders* star Jessie Wallace was the high-profile 'replacement' for Amanda. She was cast as Essex girl Amy Kriel, new wife of Elliot, a neighbour of the Trevanions. Amy finds South African life hard but has been helped to settle in by Sarah. Jessie flew out at the beginning of August 2007 with her 3-year-old daughter Tallulah and made her first appearance in Episode 5. Amanda and Jessie got on like 'a ranch on fire' and little Lexi was delighted to find a playmate in Tallulah. Amanda's final day turned out to be something of an anticlimax. There were no tears – because she had already shed them a day earlier.

'I was supposed to finish on the Monday and, of course, I went into work and cried, and everyone was crying and we were all a mess,' she recalled. 'And then I was told that filming was overrunning and I had to come back tomorrow, so I was in the next day and I had to say, "Sorry. I can't cry any more. Done that now. Not sad any more."'

After Amanda returned home she started training in earnest for her first London Marathon, which would take place the following April. Amanda was to run with her mum Judith to raise sponsorship money for the Born Free Foundation – the animal charity of which she was patron.

After three years of *Wild at Heart* she was feeling unfit, had put on an extra three pounds and was losing her muscle tone. She decided that something had to be done and, as she had always wanted to enter the London Marathon, she thought that this would provide the ideal motivation. When she told Chris, he replied, 'You're mad but you've always been a stubborn little git, so I'm sure you'll make it.'

Her initial thoughts were to take it all very casually, and

not care if she completed only half the course and then 'went for a pub lunch'. But the more she started getting in shape for the run, the more committed she became. She began by running at least 7 miles in about an hour and then managed 15 miles in just over 2 hours.

'The music on my iPod kept me going. I played "Let Me Entertain You" by Robbie Williams and my anthem, Abba's "Dancing Queen". It motivates me at every big event in my life.'

But while out jogging with her personal trainer near her Thames-side home one morning she made a shocking and macabre discovery. Around 7am they came across a man slumped at the foot of a tree beside the canal. He had a noose around his neck, which was tied to a branch. A bottle of brandy and some strong flu medicine were lying nearby. They tried to wake him but realised he was dead. Amanda ran for help while her trainer stayed with the body. She found a canal worker who rang 999, and the pair of them waited for police and an ambulance to arrive.

'I was surprisingly calm at the time,' she recalled. 'It felt very surreal. But as I walked Lexi in the park later the shock hit me, and I felt really sad for both the man and his family.'

An investigation into the death revealed that he had hanged himself from a tree before falling to the ground.

That October it was announced that Les was to become a father again at the age of 53. His girlfriend, Claire

Nicholson, 36, was due to give birth in April. Older and wiser, and regretting the way he had treated Philip, Les was going to be doing things differently this time. Meanwhile, Amanda was eagerly looking forward to working on the second series of *BGT*. She had never felt as excited with any other jobs she had done. The only drawback was that it took her away from Lexi.

When the audition stage of the show began at the end of January 2008, Amanda was heartbroken as Lexi clung to her while she was leaving the house, crying for her not to go. Whenever Lexi saw Amanda on TV, her face would light up and sometimes she would go round the back of the TV set to see if Mummy was there. Already she was showing some of Amanda's early love of performing and would pick up hairbrushes, TV remote-control consoles – or whatever came to hand – and use them as microphones.

As *BGT* got under way Amanda felt that some of Simon's ruthlessness was rubbing off on her. Previously she hated to hurt other people's feelings and avoided shattering their dreams – even if they were clearly never going to make it. And, whenever she tried to tell an act it was all over, her mouth went dry and her mind blank. But now she was dealing with it more easily. 'I've learned so much from Simon and now I'm ruthless,' she joked. 'As time goes by it gets easier.'

Meanwhile, Amanda kept in training for the London Marathon throughout the series, even though it meant having to put up with a relentlessly competitive Piers

Morgan. He would often follow her to the gym, ask the staff which machine she had been on and then try to better her time. And, when Simon sponsored Amanda £1,000 for the run, Piers pipped him with £1,001.

Amanda loved the plethora of oddball acts in the show, such as a chainsaw juggler, belly dancer and a magician whose doves flew off and never came back. She particularly enjoyed the moments when stone-faced Simon Cowell was reduced to hysterics. 'I love the fact that we are a nation of eccentric nutters. I love the fact that people have the balls to go out and perform, and have a sense of humour.' Her particular highlight of this series was an escapologist who couldn't get out of his sack and spent ten minutes staggering about in chains before he had to be cut free by the Red Cross.

As in the first series, Amanda again found it hard to keep her emotions in check. Such as when 13-year-old Andrew Johnston – dubbed the new Aled Jones – revealed how he has been bullied by classroom yobs since the age of 6 and wanted to make something of his life. A clearly moved Amanda remarked, 'I promised I wouldn't cry this series but you've made me.'

And she was close to tears when single mum Madonna Decia, 32, told how she had made the heartrending decision to leave her two children behind in the Philippines while she came to Britain for a 'better life' and to send money back home to them. As Decia launched into Whitney Houston's 'I Will Always Love You' Amanda started to blub.

Dog-loving Amanda put Gin the dancing dog through to the final and considered it to be an ideal act for the Royal Variety Performance. Among other acts to make it through to the last were Andrew Johnston, 8-year-old girl dancers the Cheeky Monkeys and 14-year-old street dancer George Sampson from Warrington.

For the final Amanda wore a Union Flag dress, which echoed the memorable outfit worn by Spice Girl Geri Halliwell at the 1997 BRIT Awards. The show made her feel proud to be British and so she wanted to fly the flag. 'I knew from the start what I wanted: something that stated what this show is all about – pride in our country and our people,' she explained. 'I think we've managed to celebrate the great things about Britain in a way that brings the country together. It doesn't matter where you're from, what colour you are or your accent. I feel I'm at the heart of a great national event.'

The winner was George Sampson, who gave a break-dancing twist to 'Singin' in the Rain', which had Amanda moist eyed once more.

Despite all the crying, Amanda had enjoyed the series even more than the first. The show had proved itself, everyone knew what they were doing and the judges forged closer ties. 'I want to be doing this show when I'm ninety and you have to wheel me on stage in a wheelchair,' she said. 'I love the job. I'd be gutted if Simon wheeled out another judge in place of me. I'd kill him.'

But she was looking forward to spending the summer at

home with her family in the new house they had bought in Richmond, Surrey, that March. For the first time in four years she had the summer free instead of being in South Africa filming *Wild at Heart*.

And, of course, there was the wedding in December. 'It's going to be a massive party with all the people we love. I can see Chris and me growing old together, except I won't look old. He'll be grey and I'll be like Joan Rivers!'

Explaining her taste in men, she said she didn't go for the obviously handsome men like Brad Pitt or Johnny Depp but preferred more unconventional looks. She preferred the likes of Jack Nicholson or maybe Owen Wilson. And Amanda knew she had found her perfect match in Chris. 'He ticks all the boxes really. He's tall, sexy, funny. He says I'm allowed to fancy Jack Nicholson if he's allowed to like Julia Roberts.' She was hoping to have another child – ideally a brother for Lexi – and said that they would probably start trying for one next year.

It had been a terrific year for her so far. *BGT* had shown her in a new light. Here was a softer, more emotional side to her character than she had previously displayed in public. Indeed, she had been at pains to hide such traits behind a cheery smile and a belief that 'the show must go on'. Now she was more relaxed and felt able to wear her heart on her sleeve, and the public had warmed to her.

'There was an affair and I was labelled a man's woman, which stayed with me for years,' she said. 'The truth is I enjoy flirting but I was never a man eater. When a woman makes a mistake, it's hard to shift the stigma but, thanks to *Britain's Got Talent*, things have changed. I've been able to be me and people have changed their opinions – especially women. I'm not a minx really. Well, only with my husband!'

But the publication of Les Dennis's autobiography, *Must The Show Go On?*, in March 2008 dug up the past once more. Much of it was less than flattering about his former wife and she was furious with him.

Amanda knew that Les was writing the book and, although she was a little apprehensive about his dragging up the past and what he would say, she felt there was no bad feeling between them, that they had both moved on and that he would be fair. But Les poured out the last of his pent-up emotions and went into considerable detail about the events surrounding 'the affair', how she behaved and how it made him feel.

Les revealed how Amanda had talked about Neil Morrissey to him after they had worked together on *Happy Birthday Shakespeare*. In the wake of the affair they tried to patch things up on their wedding anniversary but Les said he was shocked when she casually mentioned that she paid for dinner with Neil the night before with Les's credit card.

Les conceded that Amanda might not be happy with the book but he thought it was a fair and honest account of what happened and how he felt. 'I really wanted to be honest about what had happened but I also didn't want to just stick the knife in,' he said. 'But it's difficult not to.' However, he thought it was balanced because he also talked about his own failings, including his misery, 'cowardice' and 'adultery' – when he cheated on his first wife, Lynne.

Recalling the newspaper frenzy during the height of the Amanda-and-Neil affair, Les told the *Guardian*, 'It was a red-top [tabloid newspaper] gift. There were three people who were pretty well known. Amanda was on the ascent. I was telly wallpaper and, to some people, the Norman Maine-type failing celebrity and Neil Morrissey was the bad boy. It just kept on going.'

The Norman Maine reference was apt. In the classic movie *A Star Is Born* movie star Maine helps a young singer/actress find fame, as age and alcoholism send his own career into obscurity and suicide. Amanda's affair with Neil was to turn the public against her, while Les became what she once described as 'a national treasure'. The book revealed how, in the middle of the crisis, Les's old pal Bob Monkhouse phoned to offer support. But it was cold comfort. Les rewatched footage of his time in *Celebrity Big Brother* while researching and was mortified by his embarrassing antics. In a *Guardian* interview to publicise his autobiography Les said that he no longer speaks to Amanda. 'She wanted us to talk and I just thought you've got to let those things go.' Although he expected her to be upset about certain things in the book, he was unrepentant. He said he knew there would be things she wouldn't like. The writing of the book had been a cathartic experience for Les but he felt another chapter opening in his life with the arrival of his and Claire's baby, Eleanor Grace, on 24 April 2008.

'People still like to think of me as sad, lonely Les but I'm not. I'm now the happiest and most contented I've ever been in my life.' Then, using a line from the opening sentence of L.P. Hartley's book, *The Go-Between*, he added, 'The past is a foreign country.'

As the day of the London Marathon approached Amanda had set herself a target of completing the race in under four and a half hours. Whatever happened, the months of training had given her the determination to cross the finishing line, even if it meant walking. In the event, a delighted Amanda cracked it in 4 hours, 13 minutes, 22 seconds.

Amanda's ultra-smooth complexion – seen in close-up as the camera zoomed in on her in *BGT* – had been the topic of much conversation in the press, and in offices and factories, and at dinner tables around the country. She was 37 but there seemed to be a complete absence of any wrinkle. Did she just have good genes or was she having a little help? A picture of her in a newspaper appeared to show her with unusually large lips. Had they been enhanced? Amanda eventually admitted that she had been having Botox and had the first injections in 2007 after the fierce African sun caused her to have wrinkles while filming *Wild at Heart*.

'I was constantly frowning in the sun and I noticed crow's feet coming, and that's when I had it,' she said. But she categorically denied having had anything done to her lips, insisting that they were getting thinner rather than plumper.

Following the publication of Les's autobiography Amanda felt compelled to talk to newspapers about her side of the story and how badly the backlash from the affair had affected her. Looking back, she could see that, when she married Les, not everybody believed she loved him because of the age gap and his fame. 'They were waiting for something to happen. Our relationship lasted for ten years, which isn't bad considering I met him when I was twenty-two. I should have been out there having a wild time like all the other girls my age but I wasn't. I was going home every night to what was, initially, a very happy marriage. Then I had the affair and everything went mad.'

Hoping to draw a final line under the issue, she added, 'There are no hard feelings with Les. I wish him the best but we've both moved on.'

SIXTEEN

MARRIAGE – AND AMERICA AT LAST!

'I can't wait to call him my husband.'
AMANDA HOLDEN ON CHRIS HUGHES

D espite having expressed regret that she and Les Dennis had lived their life so much in the public eye and that having their wedding and an 'At Home' feature in *OK!* magazine was a mistake, Amanda Holden did a U-turn when she sold the rights to her forthcoming wedding to the same magazine.

Her hen night was, of course, organised by her best friend, Sarah Parish. But wild nights out clubbing in London were a thing of the past. Instead, the hen party of 9 went to Amanda and Chris's favourite hotel and restaurant in Burnham Market, Norfolk – the 17th-century coaching inn, Hoste Arms. Among those invited were fellow actors Angela Griffin and Lisa Faulkner. Here they enjoyed fine champagne and fine dining, strolled around the picturesque village and went for invigorating walks in the countryside and on the beach.

Chris's stag do was more exotic. It was organised by his best man, Formula 1 driver David Coulthard, who took the 14-strong party to Monaco, where they stayed at the Columbus Hotel, which he owns. It turned into quite an event. The World Music Awards were on at that time so the whole place was buzzing with musicians, celebrities and glamorous people.

David had a few traditional stag surprises for Chris – much to his embarrassment. The party went to an upmarket restaurant, and Chris was mortified when two strippers arrived and started shedding their clothes in front of the well-to-do diners. 'It was like having strippers at The Ivy!' he recalled. 'One couple were in there and the woman walked out, and her husband just sat there in shock.'

Amanda was eagerly looking forward to the wedding and to be able to call Chris her husband at long last. 'I can't wait to call him my husband. I hate the word "partner" and "fiancé" just sounds stupid. "Husband" is much cooler.'

Amanda ended up with three wedding rings because she couldn't choose which she liked best! While in South Africa she saw a ring she liked with lots of diamonds and, although Chris thought it a little ostentatious, he bought it for her. But then she saw another ring that Chris liked too and so he bought that. But it didn't stop there.

While working on *Britain's Got Talent* she got talking to representatives from a diamond company and fell in love with a ring they showed her. It had two diamond bands, which could be joined together to fit an engagement ring inside. Chris ended up buying that too and this was the ring that he was eventually to put on her finger.

Two days before the wedding a small group of men – including Chris, David, Piers Morgan and Mick Hucknall – had dinner at a restaurant in Bath, where David admitted he was nervous about the best man's speech. 'Stick me on a hundred-and-sixty-mile-per-hour hairpin at Monaco any time over making speeches.'

The wedding at Babington House included celebrity guests such as F1 racing driver Jenson Button, Sarah Parish, Mick Hucknall, Noddy Holder, Piers Morgan, Anita Dobson, Russ Abbott, Angela Griffin, Lisa Faulkner and Jessie Wallace. A notable absence was Amanda's *BGT* boss Simon Cowell. Amanda later explained, 'He has some big music event to go to but Piers Morgan is coming. I don't think Simon can bear weddings. Mind you, there are so many gags about him in the speeches that it's best that he's not there because I'd be sacked!'

Ever the one for the camp and theatrical, Amanda pulled out all the stops to make this a day to remember. Amanda appeared at 4pm as her favourite song, Abba's 'Dancing Queen', belted out over the sound system. It was an entrance so camp that she couldn't resist it.

Her champagne-coloured wedding dress would be kept

for Lexi to marry in. She teamed it with six-inch heels, vintage earrings and a diamond bracelet given to her by Chris. In return, she gave him a vintage 1927 Rolex.

Chris, dressed in a black velvet suit, stood with his best man David Coulthard at the foot of the altar, looking as anxious and excited as any other groom. A snow machine was put to work outside the church and, as the church doors opened, the guests walked out into a winter wonderland. Father Christmas arrived on his sleigh, along with his two reindeer and elves, who gave out presents to the children. The youngsters were then whisked away to enjoy a party of their own while the couple posed for photographs. Then they headed back to the House for speeches and the feast of a lifetime.

When it came to Chris's speech, he thanked everyone for 'coming to watch me become Mr Amanda Holden in this amazing location'. There was a break before the best man's speech, which, despite David Coulthard's nervousness, had the guests marvellously entertained. The happy couple's 'first dance' was to the Boyzone song 'Better'. All their months of planning had paid off. It was the perfect wedding that they had hoped for.

Amanda and Chris delayed their honeymoon for a few weeks so that they could enjoy a family Christmas at home. Then, towards the end of December 2008, they were off to the Maldives for a luxurious nine-day stay at a top health spa, while Lexi stayed with Amanda's mum, Judith, in Cornwall. The happy couple relaxed in a house by the sea, with beautiful white beaches all around them, and ate fresh fish and drank cocktails. 'It was like something out of a Bounty advert,' Amanda later recalled. 'From our room you walked down straight to the ocean and in the spa the floor was glass, so, when you were face down having your massage, you were looking at tropical fish.' A private butler was on hand to cater for their every needs and they had the use of a 70-foot yacht.

Deliriously happy, they returned home but Amanda was brought back to earth just a few days later when she was about to start work on the third series of *Britain's Got Talent*. Simon Cowell phoned her to say that shapely model turned actress Kelly Brook would be joining them as a fourth judge.

Amanda was actually in the car travelling to Manchester for the first audition when she got the call from Simon. She admits to being shocked and cross at both the late notification and the decision. She knew exactly what Simon was playing at. He had set up a rival clash on *The X Factor* by bringing in gorgeous Cheryl Cole to sit alongside Dannii Minogue as a judge. Now he was obviously trying the same ploy again.

The newspapers loved the idea of an older woman being incensed by the arrival of a younger and stunningly beautiful rival but Amanda promptly played down any sense of jealousy. 'This is what the press wanted. I don't understand how anyone could fall into that trap when there are big bright lights saying, "Jump in here and be a bitch". That's not me and Kelly's got no side to her either,' she stormed.

Kelly was delighted to be joining the high-profile show, saying that she had been a huge fan since the first series and she couldn't wait to start watching the acts. Simon commented, 'Kelly is great fun – and has absolutely no idea what she's let herself in for.' This was undoubtedly true, as she could never have imagined what would happen just days later. But for the moment she excitedly threw herself into things and turned heads when she arrived in Manchester in a slinky black dress and high heels. Not to be out-glammed, Amanda looked dramatic in a pencil-thin black dress and red stilettos.

The 'battle of the beauties' took a comical turn two days later when they appeared in almost identical outfits. Kelly was in a white high-necked dress and high-heeled beige Christian Louboutin No Barre shoes. Then, much to the newspapers' delight, Amanda emerged in a remarkably similar dress with the same shoes but in black. And both had red nail polish on their toes.

Simon was amused when the gathered reporters told him about it. 'Are they both wearing white dresses? I love that!' He grinned like the cat that had got the cream. 'I think they're trying to outdress each other. You know what girls are like.'

But just six days into the job came the shock news that Kelly had been axed. Simon, who had once again generated maximum publicity at the start of the series, explained that having four judges was 'too complicated'. Amanda was gracious about Kelly but said that having four judges was unworkable and even baffled the show's hosts, Ant and Dec. 'Kelly's a lovely girl but it doesn't work with four people because, when two buzz and two don't, Ant and Dec and everyone was going, "What does that mean?" It was so ridiculously confusing. It was a shame for her because she was thrown completely in at the deep end.'

Once more she stressed that there was no friction or resentment between them. 'I know everyone expected Kelly and me to be mud-wrestling at dawn when she was put on the panel but we genuinely got on well. I didn't feel my position had been undermined in any way. As to why she departed so quickly afterwards, I haven't the smallest idea. Simon didn't consult me but then he wouldn't. He's the boss. I'm a panellist.'

Even mischievous gossip monger Piers Morgan poured cold water on the suggestion that there was any rivalry between the girls. 'They are both nice people,' he said. 'Amanda's not a bitchy girl and was cool with Kelly.' Once more it was the three judges – and now good friends – back together like old times. And such was the friendship between them that, when Simon was invited to 10 Downing Street to meet the then Prime Minister Gordon Brown, he took Amanda and Piers with him. 'He was too shy to go on his own,' Amanda explained.

Despite the team's concerns that they might run out of

variety acts now the show was in its third year, the country rose to the challenge. And Amanda thought the auditions were the most entertaining they had ever had. She often had a tummy ache at the end of the day because she had been laughing so much.

Among the novelty acts was a man who swung dustbins from his ears and a transvestite belly dancer. But the biggest eye-opener was dancer Fabia Cerra. She came on stage looking quite respectable in a black dress and red feather boa. After she demurely thanked Simon for giving her the chance to show what she could do, he smiled and murmured to his co-judges, 'She's sweet.' But none of them had any idea of what was to come next.

As 'The Stripper' played Simon looked horrified. A shimmering Fabia turned her back, removed her black jacket and then, wearing just a basque, turned to reveal she was wearing nipple tassels! Simon looked as if he wanted the floor to swallow him up but the audience, and Amanda and Piers, thought it hilarious. By the end Amanda had laughed so much that her sides were hurting. 'I nearly had to be carried off in an ambulance. I am utterly speechless.'

Simon, too, had seen the funny side and all three of them voted her through. When the moment was screened on TV, Union Flags were digitally positioned over her assets!

Less than entertaining was James Boyd, 33, from Dunfermline, who wanted to beat the current world record for eating Ferrero Rocher chocolates in a minute, which currently stood at seven. Everyone thought that seven didn't sound that impressive but James said he had been practising for the last seven months. As a bored-looking Simon held a stopwatch James started his 'act'. Meanwhile, backstage, Ant was also having a go while Dec timed him. By the end of the minute, James had eaten the grand total of four. Ant had managed five! Amanda gave James a withering look and commented, 'I honestly think I could have done better than that.'

The unforgettable moment of the series was when unemployed church volunteer Susan Boyle, from Blackburn in West Lothian, walked onto the stage. Awkward, nervous and far from glamorous, as Simon raised his eyeballs she described her singing as being a bit like that of Elaine Paige. But as she launched into 'I Dreamed a Dream' from the musical *Les Misérables* jaws dropped all around the studio.

A tearful Amanda told her it was a 'complete privilege' to listen to her singing. Susan – or 'SuBo' as she was to become nicknamed – became an Internet sensation via website YouTube and won over America. Even Hollywood actress Demi Moore announced she was a big fan.

Another of Amanda's favourite acts – and another that had her crying but this time with laughter – was the father-and-son novelty act Stavros Flatley, who mixed a peculiar blend of Greek and Irish dance to brilliant comic effect.

The bickering between Amanda and Piers increased this series but it was only because they were now like brother and sister, and enjoyed the cut and thrust of banter and one-upmanship. And their habit of relaxing off camera in the hotel bar after the show continued, once their 'headmaster' Simon Cowell had departed. 'Piers and I will go to the bar for a beer and a sarnie after the show, while Simon is off on the phone to LA – he never socialises with us,' said Amanda.

But she did admit to having developed a schoolgirl-type crush on Simon. 'Simon's good friends with the hypnotist Paul McKenna, and I think he eases you into his psyche because you do end up finding him utterly charming and very funny.' She also divulged some secret games that Simon liked to play on the show, such as whispering to his colleagues that they should get a random word such as 'lettuce' into their next sentence.

As the show reached the semi-final stage there were concerns that Susan Boyle would crack under the pressure following her sensational first performance. But she again brought the audience to its feet with a stunning performance of 'Memory'. The show drew a remarkable 15.4 million viewers.

Simon Cowell was moved to apologise, although he wasn't about to shoulder all of the blame. 'You are one special lady,' he told her. 'I want to apologise for the way we treated you the first time you sang. You made me and everyone else look stupid.'

Before the *BGT* final on 30 May 2009 there was the FA Cup final earlier in the day, which Amanda and Chris attended, between Chris's beloved Everton and Chelsea.

Amanda wore a blue dress to support their side but they lost 2–1.

That evening hot favourite Susan Boyle – now known around the world – once more sang 'I Dreamed a Dream'. It looked as if her dream was about to come true until it was announced that the energetic dance troupe Diversity were that year's winners. Not that it mattered much anyway. She got a record contract and was invited to America to appear on, among others, *The Oprah Winfrey Show*.

Amanda was highly amused when she learned that Simon would be spending Christmas with his ex-girlfriends Sinitta, Jackie St Claire and Terri Seymour. But the more she got to know the real person, the more she understood his appeal. 'Simon is one of the most charming, self-effacing and lovely men I know. Yes, he acts flash but he's just giving people what they want. And he hates rudeness. He's just brutally honest. He has this magnetism. I don't know why. But apparently he's never changed and I'll tell you what: his opinions are great, his advice is good, he's very practical and he's very generous. And just utterly himself.'

He may not have been interested in 'domestic issues' but Amanda valued his advice on the professional front. And he encouraged her to be herself. As for Piers Morgan, he was the one she could discuss family matters with. 'In many ways I have a more honest relationship with Piers. He's a family man and understands all the chaos that goes with that. So he doesn't glaze over when I tell him something funny Lexi said last week. I tease Piers all the time – and vice versa.'

The day after the first *BGT* show of the season went out on TV Chris received a call from the US to say that his father, Mike, 72, had been involved in a serious car crash. He was on holiday and had been walking near Sunset Boulevard when a delivery truck veered out of control and hit two parked cars. The force of the smash flipped one over, which hurtled into Mike, trapping him underneath. Mike didn't have any identification on him, so doctors had to wait until he woke from his coma to find out who he was. It took two days, therefore, before Chris received the horrifying news.

Chris and Amanda rushed to Los Angeles to be by his side in intensive care. They were shocked to see the state he was in. He had multiple facial injuries, and broken ribs and cuts. But, amazingly, he made a good recovery and was discharged two weeks later, and the three of them returned home.

Much as she was enjoying herself as a judge on *BGT*, Amanda didn't want to put all her eggs in one basket and thought it time to do some comedy acting once again. And earlier in the year she signed up to star in a new TV comedy series called *Big Top*. In this she played Lizzie, the ring mistress of Circus Maestro. A strong cast included John Thomson from the comedy drama series *Cold Feet* as a clown and *Blackadder* star Tony Robinson as a cynical soundman.

'It's a bit like *Britain's Got Talent* in a way because it has so many random acts in it,' Amanda explained. 'But it is also a bit of a cross between the *Vicar of Dibley* and *Hi-De-Hi!*'

In fact, Ruth Madoc, who played Gladys Pugh in the hit 1980s sitcom *Hi-De-Hi!*, was also in *Big Top* as veteran performer Georgie, the Grande Dame of Circus Maestro, who performs with her Scottie dog. Amanda – for reasons hard to fathom – saw all this in a positive light.

'It's credit-crunch comedy,' she said in a reference to the buzz phrase of the difficult economic times. 'It's such an obvious idea; it's amazing it's never been done before. Most comedies now seem to be set in someone's lounge or house, with a washing machine, a pet and two kids. But, in the climate we're in, it's just great that before we even open our mouths there's something fantastic to look at. There's a huge circus tent, clowns, people dressed up, and loads of colour and eccentricity. It's bums-on-seats comedy, it's family entertainment.'

Well, that was one opinion. Unfortunately, few people saw the joke and, when the show went out in December, it fell flat on its face like a circus clown.

'It has an authentic circus atmosphere – it reeks like a ring full of elephant dung,' said the *Daily Star* scathingly. The *Stage* said the jokes were 'limp and lumbered with punch lines Nostradamus probably saw coming', while the *Observer* called it 'unashamedly lame'.

But Amanda had long ago learned how to shake off such criticism and, ever willing to try new things, she had a five-week crash course to learn how to be a midwife for a documentary called *Out of My Depth* in which she helped to deliver babies. It was, she says, 'an emotional experience and a huge responsibility'.

The programme was well received and was to spark off another idea four months later.

Just 48 hours after the dramatic final of *BGT* Amanda flew out to the US to be interviewed on the CBS morning programme, *The Early Show*. And there was only one person they wanted to talk to her about: Susan Boyle. She also appeared on the prestigious *Larry King Live* show.

She proved to be so popular that she was asked to come back to do some presenting. An excited Amanda sensed that the moment she had been waiting for all these years was actually happening. After doing some presenting slots she was signed up as UK entertainment correspondent on *The Early Show*.

For the past 15 years Amanda had gone to LA for weeks every year, and had loads of screen tests and agonising near misses, such as almost being a Bond girl. Then she married and had a baby, and her priorities changed but she never let go of her American dream. Now, when she wasn't expecting it, she had cracked America at last. It wasn't how she had originally planned – through acting – but that seemed not to matter. And she knew whom she owed it to. 'I'll be the first to say that it was all because of Susan. The US networks couldn't get enough of the SuBo story, and CBS kept interviewing Piers Morgan and me about what was happening. Somewhere along the way they seemed to like me too.'

Now she was making regular trips across the Atlantic and taking her family with her as much as possible. She loved the buzz of New York but knew that she could never live there. She loved England too much.

Following the success of *Out of My Depth* Amanda started work on a three-part ITV1 series in September 2009 called *Amanda Holden's Fantasy Lives*, in which she tried her hands at different professions: a Paris showgirl, a stuntwoman and a country singer. At the famous Moulin Rouge in Paris she was snootily informed that her legs were not long enough to be allowed to dance on their stage and, at five feet, four inches, she was three inches too short for the minimum height. So she headed off to the Lido club on the Champs-Elysées, home to the world-renowned Bluebell Girls. Although all the girls here were over five feet, eight inches, Amanda was allowed to dance with them but found learning the moves incredibly difficult and strenuous. Despite being racked with nerves, she managed to put in an accomplished performance, wearing a glitzy pink satin costume, fishnet tights and diamante G-string.

But Amanda's favourite experience in the series was

trying her hand at being a Hollywood stuntwoman. She always resented it when stunt doubles took over from her for action scenes in her various acting jobs but now she could do it herself and loved throwing herself off buildings onto mattresses, crashing cars into boxes and doing 90- and 180-degree handbrake turns.

For the final show she went to Texas, experienced life on a ranch and got some singing tips from Kenny Rogers before performing a couple of country and western songs at the famous Broken Spoke dance hall.

Between filming commitments she fitted in time to attend Simon Cowell's 50th-birthday party. Cowell, who hides his shyness behind a mask of confidence, dislikes parties as much as weddings. And being the centre of attention at his own party was hellish for him but he agreed to the celebration under pressure from former girlfriend Sinitta. 'He said it was the first and last party he'd have to celebrate a birthday. He really hates fuss,' said Sinitta.

'It's daunting for him. He really does hate being the centre of attention. When he's on *The X Factor* it's a stage persona but off screen he's a people watcher. He loves sitting back and knowing his friends are having a good time. But he hates people making a fuss over him.'

The party took place at Wrotham Park, a stately manor in Barnet, Hertfordshire. Among the 400 guests were Jennifer Lopez, Naomi Campbell, Kate Moss, Ant and Dec, Sharon and Ozzy Osbourne, Alexandra Burke, Kelly Brook, Alan Sugar, Gordon and Tana Ramsay, Elton

John, Kevin Spacey, Andrew Lloyd Webber, Cheryl Cole and Piers Morgan. They were treated to performances from Westlife and the 2007 *X Factor* winner Leona Lewis. Amanda described the occasion as 'the party of the decade'. It was, she said, a mix of decadence and fun with great attention to detail, including name plates with cherubs wearing G-strings and gold crowns.

But she was bemused by one of the cabaret acts, who had flown over from a New York nightclub, which she described as being 'dancers dressed as female genitalia'. Simon was taken aback too. He was particularly embarrassed and uncomfortable because he was sitting next to his mother.

Wondering what present to buy the man who has everything, Amanda decided on a jokey one: a signed photo of herself in a silver frame and also a silver champagne bucket.

In November, while in LA filming the stuntwoman episode of *Fantasy Lives*, Amanda discovered a lump in her groin. A doctor was called on set to take a look and Amanda took the opportunity to mention the thing that she had tried to put to the back of her mind: the lump she had found on her breast six months earlier. She had meant to have it checked out but could never quite find the time. But she was shocked by what was to come.

SEVENTEEN

CANCER SCARE AND FAMILY MATTERS

'Life's precious. We should do all we can to keep it.'
AMANDA HOLDEN AFTER HER CANCER SCAN

Amanda Holden had first felt a lump on her right breast when she was at home checking herself in May 2009. She noticed a small round ball that moved beneath her fingers but she wasn't overly worried. She had recently had a private medical examination, which included MRI scans, brain scans and kidney, liver and blood tests, and the results had come back fine. So she put the lump down to a blocked milk duct because she hadn't breastfed Lexi as a baby.

That night she asked Chris if he could check the lump for her. Although he could feel something, he assured her that it would be nothing serious but he suggested she see a doctor to put her mind at rest. Chris's words of comfort reassured her and, although she agreed to make an appointment, she didn't get round to it. 'Like many women, I'm so busy it's easy to ignore health issues because there's just no time to think about them,' she said. 'I put the lump to the back of my mind. I kept thinking that, the next time I needed a health check for work, I'd get someone to have a look.'

That moment came six months later in LA. Amanda wasn't prepared for the worst. On the contrary, she was sure that all would be fine. 'I was jovial when I approached the doctor, as I thought he was going to tell me the lump was nothing to worry about. But, when he said I needed to get it checked out at hospital right away, I felt sick.' After booking an appointment for the next morning she tried to carry on as normal but she just couldn't stop thinking about it and the stunt scenes that she had been enjoying so much suddenly felt too physical. She just wanted to go home and snuggle up on the sofa.

Back in her hotel suite she longed to have Chris by her side to give her comfort but he was miles away, back home in England. She telephoned him and again he tried to reassure her that all would be fine because of her recent private medical examination. She also called her old friend Jane Wall, now living in LA, who said she would take her to the mammogram clinic, where she had an appointment the following morning. Amanda tried to take her mind off things by watching TV and drinking half a bottle of red wine. But that night as she lay in bed her mind raced with what might happen and she was highly emotional when she thought of her loved ones.

'My mind dwelled on silly things like who would take Lexi to birthday parties. I deliberately made myself stop.' At the hospital the next morning Jane comfortingly held her hand. Amanda later vividly recalled the tense wait down to the smallest detail. 'After filling out umpteen forms I was directed to a changing room, where I put all my clothes inside a locker, then put on a backless gown before taking a seat in the waiting room. I can still remember the feeling of my cold bum on the leather chair, waiting. It was horrible.

While she waited Amanda decided that, if the lump was cancerous and needed to be cut out, she would tell them to take the whole breast off. As she sat there thinking about how she would have reconstructive surgery she was called to the treatment room.

The mammogram wasn't as bad an experience as she thought it would be and she considered it more uncomfortable than painful. After that she had an agonising hour-long wait before being given the results. 'Butterflies fluttered around my tummy and my heart was pounding as I waited for the news. I was thinking, Just give it to me because I knew that I would deal with whatever was coming.'

When the doctor told her that the results were clear and that lump was just a collection of gristle-like tissue, she felt an enormous relief mingled with the feeling that she had wasted everyone's time. But afterwards she was angry with herself for feeling that way. 'That's what women need to stop worrying about. You're not wasting your doctor's time. If you're worried about your health, you must get checked out. Just pick up the phone and make an appointment. As women, we need to think about how loved ones would cope if we weren't around. Life's precious. We should do all we can to keep it.'

The scare made Amanda appreciate her family even more and she was determined to enjoy every moment with them.

Earlier that year Amanda had realised that being a busy working mum had been much more stressful than she thought it would be. One day in July, after the family had driven to their home in Norfolk, she unexpectedly burst into tears the moment she walked through the front door. 'I think it was sheer exhaustion,' she later recalled. 'It's only when I stopped that I realised what I'd put myself through that year. I don't have a nanny – Lexi is looked after by me, Chris and our mums. I think every mum knows how I was feeling: you're doing all you can to be perfect and then you stop, look at your child and think, How could I have done it better?'

Like any working mum, she felt guilty about not being with her child enough and so the sweetest and most innocent of Lexi's comments would make her cry. One occasion was when she was reading Lexi a story in bed. Lexi looked up at her and said, 'When I'm bigger, I'll still need you, Mummy.'

But Norfolk provided an ideal bolthole for Amanda to spend quality time with both Lexi and Chris, and enjoy simple family pleasures, such as picking gooseberries with Lexi to make jam, baking cakes and going to the seaside. 'If everything went wrong in my career, I'd live there for the rest of my life,' she later stated. 'It's the only place in the world where I relax.'

Her regular bouts of crying on *BGT* had become something of a national joke but it was no act. Her driven and ambitious behaviour may have come across as ruthless at times but, despite her sometimes hard veneer, she had always been a very emotional person.

At home, whenever she was in tears over something relatively silly – a soppy TV show, a happy moment – she recalled how Chris would look at her and ask, 'Mandy, are you having a breakdown?' And then he would laugh. And, whenever there was a radio traffic report about a breakdown, Chris would comment, 'Yeah, I know, it's Mandy.'

It was revealed to the press that another joke among them is her nickname for him: Crispy. The name stuck after Amanda was amused by a letter that once arrived for him addressed to 'Chris P Hughes'.

She now had the transatlantic career she had always wanted but, whenever she had imagined it in the past, it had never involved having a husband and child. And the time she spent away from both of them when they were unable to be with her in the States was tough for her. It was also frustrating that she was unable to find the time to try for another child.

'I've always thought I'd love Lexi to have a brother or sister. But to have children you have to have sex and I've gone sixteen days without even seeing my husband!' she said at the time.

In her calmer moments, however, she didn't feel any real pressure to have a second baby. She would be 39 on her next birthday and, while she thought it would be nice if she did fall pregnant again, she reconciled herself to the fact that she had a beautiful and healthy girl, and so anything else would just be a bonus.

She was as madly in love with Chris as ever. Occasionally, she said, she would look at him and think, Oh my God, I can't believe I'm with you. You're so handsome.

For the most part, life at home with Chris was full of fun. 'He's very funny and he's always very upbeat and happy, as am I, so that works great together,' she said in interview. But she had Chris blushing in an interview she did with *Glamour* magazine. During a series of personal questions she was asked to name the strangest place she'd ever made love. Amanda didn't flinch but immediately replied, 'In a tiny little forest in Maidenhead. I was wearing pink cowboy boots and poor Chris has still got the scars on his knees.'

On one occasion Chris joined Amanda in LA and they went for dinner with Simon Cowell. Also at the table was the Hollywood actress Kate Hudson, who started talking about how she liked museums and art. When she asked a jetlagged Chris what he liked to do, he replied, 'My favourite thing is stinking in bed watching telly.' Amanda was highly amused but Kate's face was a picture. She didn't know whether to be shocked or laugh, or be revolted.

That November of 2009 Les Dennis married Claire Nicholson. In stark contrast to Amanda and Chris's wedding, Les turned down magazine offers to cover the occasion. And it was an intimate affair, with their 19-month-old daughter Eleanor as flower girl. They exchanged vows at a church ceremony at St Augustine of Canterbury Church in Highgate, north London. Afterwards the couple and their guests were taken by a Routemaster bus to the reception held at a nearby restaurant.

There was a sprinkling of some of Les's celebrity friends, including Lionel Blair, Michelle Collins and *Loose Women* presenters Carol McGiffin, Sherrie Hewson and Denise Welch. Amanda had not seen Les for six years but her attitude towards him had changed. 'In some ways I've always admired him for the way he doesn't try to hide his real emotions,' she said. 'He's honest about how he feels. My trouble is that I'm a people pleaser. I might feel down in the dumps but I'll always put on a bright face for the rest of the world. And I'm ruled by my heart, not my head. I always have been and it gets me into trouble. I'm not an enigma. I've wished all my life that I could be mysterious. But I ain't.'

In a mainstream family show, the like of which Les Dennis might have done years earlier, she co-hosted a TV special with Ronan Keating called *Celebrating The Carpenters*. It marked 40 years since the release of Karen and Richard Carpenter's debut album, and artists including Chrissie Hynde, Beverley Knight, Jamie Cullum and Girls Aloud's Kimberley Walsh sang their interpretations of Carpenters hits.

Amanda finished that year by joining Philip Schofield to co-host the *Sun* newspaper's annual tribute to Britain's servicemen and women, the *Sun* Military Awards, at London's Imperial War Museum. The awards, commonly know as the Millies, had half the audience in tears on the night, so Amanda was in good company!

Fifty-five nominees, with their families, comrades and many of Britain's most famous faces gathered for the ceremony. Among celebrity guests were David Jason, Michael Ball, Vera Lynn, Barbara Windsor, Ray Winstone, Rupert Grint, Michelle Collins, Keeley Hawes, Richard Wilson, Kym Marsh, William Roache and Bruce Forsyth. Princes William and Harry were among those presenting awards and a memorable moment was when Prince Harry spontaneously hugged Band of Mothers campaigner Jane Whitehouse when she wept for her lost son.

Among others honoured was a reservist sailor who left his job as a cabbie in Birmingham to board a Royal Navy ship to spend 6 months battling pirates off the coast of

Somalia. He twice played a key role in stopping attackers from taking 2 merchant vessels and, in later action, he helped to free 13 Yemeni fishermen being held hostage in the treacherous waters. Afterwards he went back to his job as a cabbie.

Also on the roll of honour was a 22-year-old marine who won the Overcoming Adversity award after he became the first double amputee to run the London Marathon after losing an arm and leg in an Afghan blast.

There were some lighter moments on the night and Amanda had everyone giggling when she announced the presenters for the first award as Spice Girls Geri Halliwell and Emma 'Bunion' – instead of Bunton.

At the end of an emotional night Amanda commented, 'It puts everything into perspective. You're thinking about Christmas and shopping, and all silly things at this time of year, and to see the bravery and achievement of these guys is incredibly humbling.'

EIGHTEEN

NEW FACES

'I will obviously really miss the boys. . .'
AMANDA HOLDEN ON PIERS MORGAN
AND SIMON COWELL

The overindulgences of eating and drinking at Christmas clearly had no effect on Amanda as, come January 2010, she was pictured in the *Daily Mail* paddling in the sea in a revealing red-and-white polka-dot two-piece. Amanda, Chris and Lexi had a lovely family holiday soaking up the sun on the Caribbean island of Antigua before she was due to return to start working on the fourth series of *Britain's Got Talent*.

Tired of all the newspaper talk about her having Botox, she regretted the fact that she admitted to having the injections and decided not to have any more.

For her 39th birthday in February 2010 Chris surprised her with dinner at The Ivy restaurant and invited along some of her pals, including Sarah Parish and Angela

Griffin. Later that month came the not unexpected news that *Big Top* had been axed. Although she might well have been disappointed that it had not been a success, she wouldn't have had time to sit back and worry about it because she had already started work on the fourth series of *Britain's Got Talent*. And she was relieved that, this time, Simon had no surprise additions to the judging panel. 'Luckily, it was the three of us this year. But we did say to Simon, "Are there any changes you would like us to know about?" As it happened, there was one addition and that was Mezhgan.'

Simon had got engaged to make-up artist Mezhgan Hussainy on Valentine's Day. They had first met on the set of the US talent series *American Idol*, in which Simon was a judge, and had been dating for a year. Amanda was delighted that he had taken the plunge and she reckoned that being in love had softened up TV's 'Mr Nasty'. It also meant that her working hours had become a little more relaxed.

'We basically started later because Simon was clearly not getting out of bed. He would often rock up at two or three in the afternoon! He's ridiculously love-struck by her, he's a complete puppy. We watched acts on the show and he kept leaning back and asking her opinion on what she thought. Then, in the green room, he would sit with his arm around her like he's thirteen years old. It's so cute!'

Amanda was very fond of Mezhgan and said they'd immediately bonded. 'Mezhgan is fantastic, she's a real girls' girl. She'll compliment us on what we're wearing and I love girls like that because that's the kind of girl I am. I thought, She can be in the gang, she's absolutely smashing.'

The auditions for *BGT* kicked off in Glasgow and, even though this was now the fourth series, Amanda was as excited as ever. It had become a definite highlight in her calendar and any other job had to fit around her commitment to it.

'I've been waiting for this since last year,' she told the crowd of 3,000 wannabes and supporters as she arrived at the Scottish Exhibition and Conference Centre.

It wasn't long before Amanda and Piers were laughing uproariously once more. This time it was when a performing horse defecated on the stage. But Simon was not amused. 'He hates toilet humour or anything like that so he was very uncomfortable,' Amanda explained.

Simon was taken ill with flu as the show moved to Birmingham and the *X Factor* judge Louis Walsh stood in for him. 'It feels like teacher's off and I can mess about a bit today,' Amanda said, laughing. Walsh, then 57, who was a big fan of the show, thoroughly enjoyed some of the more bizarre novelty acts, particularly 75-year-old Irish dancer Jimmy Ford from County Mayo, who dressed as a leprechaun, and whose props included a rainbow and a pot of gold. Amanda was later to admit that both she and Louis had fun at the absent Simon's expense by approving acts that they knew would annoy him.

But there was a clash between Louis and the

ultra-competitive Piers Morgan when Louis was made temporary head judge. Louis said that Piers had 'no qualifications' to be a talent-show judge, while Piers replied that Louis just 'giggled like a fawning leprechaun'.

But, as usual, it was nothing more than banter that served to provide good publicity for the show. And Amanda confided, 'There really wasn't any animosity behind the scenes. Piers said he didn't know why Louis said that but he felt he had to get him back. It's not wise to insult Piers. He'll always win because he's much better with words.'

Novelty acts included Persephone Lewis, who used a hosepipe, teapot and rubber glove as a musical instrument while wearing a penguin glove puppet. There was also a dancing dog called Chandi, burper Paul Hunn, strippers the Cheeky Boys and a parrot called Max, who was fed mashed potato from a fork!

Shortly after the *BGT* auditions Amanda was delighted to find that she was pregnant. Again she and Chris kept it a secret at such an early stage but at least now she didn't have to cope with the heat, bumpy terrain and exhaustion of working in Africa. Meanwhile, as people up and down the country waited expectantly for Simon, Amanda and Piers to return to the screen with the first show of the new series, everyone was talking about the 'Big Three'. Who would be the most impressive and say all the rights things, and who would lose out in the war of words? With millions of viewers eagerly waiting to scrutinise their behaviour under the spotlight, their nerves were jangling. This was history in the making – the UK's first ever televised prime-ministerial debate between Labour's Gordon Brown, Conservative leader David Cameron and Lib Dem leader Nick Clegg.

Hosted by Alastair Stewart and shown prime time from 8.30pm to 10pm on ITV1, the first of three televised debates attracted an impressive 9.4 million viewers, toppling the big soap series *Coronation Street* and *EastEnders* to become the most watched programme of the day.

That weekend there was a mini-heat wave, with temperatures hitting a high of 18.4°C (65°F) on the Saturday. As the stench of barbecues filled the air in gardens all over the country, it didn't stop a staggering 12.2 million from scuttling back inside their living rooms at 8pm to watch the first in the new series of *BGT*. It was a record audience for the opening show, proving it had lost none of its popularity.

Amanda, who wanted the show to go on for ever, was delighted and a smug Piers commented, 'I'm very pleased to discover that Simon, Amanda and I are still marginally more popular than Gordon Brown, David Cameron and Nick Clegg.'

Piers, who was due to marry novelist Celia Walden in a low-key ceremony in June, said he was not Amanda Holden and certainly wouldn't be having either *OK!* or *Hello!* magazine present. He also criticised her for continually crying on the show, saying that she 'blubs more than a two-month-old baby with colic'.

Amanda knew that Piers Morgan was just trying to wind her up as usual and, playing along with the 'game', shot back, 'Piers would love to have his wedding in a magazine but, with his huge ego, he wouldn't be able to fit a photographer in the church at the same time.'

After the phenomenon that was Susan Boyle there was more pressure on *BGT* that year. Her jaw-dropping performance had been the seminal moment in the show's history. How could they top it? Amanda thought it unlikely that they would find another act that would make such a worldwide impact for at least ten years. 'We had no way of predicting that she would turn into a global phenomenon. But it's changed the nature of the show as, now, potentially, we're looking for a worldwide star. I just have to go on my gut instinct, thinking, What do I like? And what would my mum and nan like?'

In keeping with his 'Kingpin' status, Simon had his own dressing room backstage but Amanda and Piers had to share one. On one occasion Piers ambled in while Amanda was dressing to borrow a hairdryer. A near naked and shrieking Amanda scurried behind a clothes rail, much to his amusement.

'Simon's the king of the show. He has a receiving room for guests, and Piers and I share a toilet and argue about who's going to bring in the fresh bog roll!' Amanda revealed. But she joked that it was in her contract to 'suck up' to the mogul to secure her place on the show.

Ten-year-old Chloe Hickinbottom quickly became

a hot favourite when she sang 'White Cliffs of Dover'. Her surprisingly deep and mature tones earned her a standing ovation. 'I don't know what I was expecting but it wasn't that. I can't believe you have such a full voice,' said Amanda. Piers commented, 'I shut my eyes and you could have been forty or fifty years old.' And Louis Walsh – using one of his *X Factor* phrases – said, 'You were born to sing – I think you were fantastic.'

During the semi-final stage regurgitating act Stevie Starr, who was able to swallow coins, light bulbs and even goldfish before bringing them back up again, caused Amanda to panic after he asked her if she was wearing a ring. Guessing what was about to happen, she protested that she was only wearing her engagement ring but he persuaded her to hand it to him. Even Chris, watching from home, was on the edge of his seat. Stevie promptly swallowed the ring, followed by a locked padlock and the key. To everyone's amazement he regurgitated the locked padlock with her ring attached!

The whole incident was much more traumatic for Amanda than anyone, other than Chris and her close family, realised. She was feeling emotional after suffering heartbreak just days earlier, when she learned that she had miscarried at four months. But, as always with Amanda, she hid her tears behind a smile in public and carried on working.

The *BGT* final had a good variety of acts and Amanda showed off a stylish new bob haircut, and wore a low-cut ivory designer dress. Popular dance duo Twist and Pulse set the bar high as the opening act. But nerves got the better of 81-year-old singer Janey Cutler during a rendition of Edith Piaf's 'No Regrets'. Simon, however, was in a kind mood when he told her supporters that they should overlook a stuttering start to her routine, adding, 'What you have got to do is forget the first part and listen to the second.'

Dancing dog Chandi failed to wow the judges as much as she had in previous rounds and Simon said he felt the dog was a little tired. Bookies' favourite Spellbound put in a breathtaking performance with their acrobatics. Amanda was startled when one of their 13-strong team was thrown into the air behind her and soared over her head onto the stage. Drummer Kieran Gaffney, 13, also took to the air on a stage suspended above the floor.

In the end, it was Spellbound who were jumping for joy after being voted the winners. They were hailed by Simon as the 'most astonishing' thing he had seen on live television.

After the final had ended Simon spoke to the press indicating that he may not return for the *BGT* auditions next year but would maybe just join the show for the live, televised finals. 'I like the show but it takes up a hell of a lot of time,' he said. 'Sometimes you sit there watching horrific acts and you think, I can't do this any more.' This led to much speculation as to who would be joining Amanda and Piers as judges, and among the names touted were Louis Walsh and Girls Aloud singer Kimberley Walsh.

As usual, after the excitement and adrenalin of *BGT*

Amanda was left feeling somewhat deflated once it had all ended – even more so now she had to come to terms with losing the baby she was carrying. Chris suggested that she needed a hobby to lift her spirits. Not that she had much time to sit idle. She was continuing her work with *The Early Show* in the US and enjoying interviewing such stars as Cate Blanchett and Leonardo DiCaprio.

But her ambition always exceeded her achievement, despite her being aware that she could spread herself too thin. 'I would love to be a judge on a big entertainment show over in America and I'd love to be in a Bollywood movie. Although I still get drama scripts sent to me, I think in this country you're only really allowed to do one thing at a time and at the moment I'm perceived as a presenter. But I'm so happy to be in this position now.'

Earlier in the year she had managed to squeeze in yet another TV show, a two-parter called *The Door*, which she co-hosted with Chris Tarrant. Described as an extreme game show, it featured celebrities such as Dean Gaffney, Boyzone's Keith Duffy, and Frankie Sandford from the Saturdays undergoing various revolting challenges behind 'The Door'. One of the most memorable was a room filled with rotting sheep's and cows' heads with flies all over them. The key they had to find to get out of the room was hidden in one of the sheep's heads.

'At one point Chris and I had to wear gas masks because of the stench,' said Amanda. 'We were the voyeurs of the show but still had to smell it. It smelled worse than death.'

Amanda described the show, which went out on ITV1 in early April, as a cross between *The Generation Game* and the horror movie *Saw*.

In June that year Amanda's father Frank spoke to the press again about how much he missed Amanda and wished she would see him but, while their relationship remained difficult, Amanda's own relationship with her daughter was just getting better and better. And she thought that Lexi had made her a more rounded and stable individual. 'If I had any rough edges before, Lexi has smoothed them over. I get so much back from her now that she's four. She's always saying, "I really love you, Mummy," and then gives me this massive hug. It melts your heart.'

Chris had also had a good effect on her and had encouraged her to admit when she was wrong. 'I come from a very matriarchal family, all of us are leaders and the women are strong,' she said. 'Chris has kicked that out of me and I'm pleased because being a know-it-all isn't attractive.'

But even Chris couldn't persuade her that she was wrong to keep buying designer shoes costing hundreds of pounds. He would tell her that it was ridiculous and that she should save to retire but Amanda would reply that she didn't plan to retire, and that she carried on working to buy shoes.

In an interview with the *Daily Mirror* in March 2010 she said she would forgive Chris if he had an affair but not if it happened time and time again. 'It's humiliating but I think everyone deserves a second chance.' But after 16 months of wedded bliss she said that life couldn't be better with Chris and Lexi. Amanda's extended 'family' now included Fudge the family dog, Muffy the kitten and two tropical fish, whom Lexi named Simon and Piers. 'They haven't eaten each other yet,' Amanda commented a few days after getting the fish home. 'We will have to see who we flush down the toilet first.'

Despite her outgoing nature and love of parties, Amanda has always relished quiet nights at home after a busy day. And once Lexi is in bed her favourite way to relax is with a glass of Sauvignon Blanc, watching *EastEnders*. The weekend routine at their Norfolk cottage continues with long walks along Holkham beach, whatever the weather. She also enjoys browsing around the independent clothes shops in Burnham Market and having Sunday lunches at the local Hoste Arms with a roast and red wine. Amanda just eats the vegetables while her meat is wrapped up to be taken home to the dog.

But it was champagne that was popping come June 2010 after she landed a starring role in a £10 million musical version of the hit cartoon movie *Shrek*. The show, about loveable green ogre Shrek and his sweetheart Princess Fiona, had already proved a huge hit on New York's Broadway before touring cities across the States. When news came that they were planning to bring it to London's West End in May 2011, Amanda flew over to the States to audition for the role of Princess Fiona. And, to her absolute delight, she was chosen.

'I'm so excited but, best of all, my daughter Lexi is telling everyone Mama will be a Green Princess,' she said. Then, in reference to Simon and Piers, she added, 'I feel I'm perfect for the role because I've worked with two ogres for the last four years!'

That month Amanda went back to her roots when she returned to Bishop's Waltham to open the annual carnival, which she had so enjoyed when she was a child. Residents turned up in their droves to see the local girl made good. Before declaring the event open she told the crowd, 'It is such an honour. I always dreamed I would be an actress, and come back and open the fête. So now my dreams have come true. I loved living here and it's great being back.'

Later she spent three hours signing autographs and having photographs taken with a long queue of fans. Amanda's nan, Win, looked on proudly, saying, 'Amanda came to my house beforehand and made me a cup of tea. She loves meeting people like this. She has always loved acting and she was very well liked in Bishop's Waltham.'

Her former drama teacher, Angie Blackford, was also there and said, 'She's my little star. I always knew she would go on to be in the West End. I love her.'

Also that month Amanda staged a party for her good friend Paul Whittome, owner of the Hoste Arms, to cheer him up, as he had been battling cancer for the past year. Paul's hotel often attracted celebrities, and Amanda invited all his friends and got popular *Britain's Got Talent* Greek/Irish dancers Stavros Flatley to perform. And he was delighted when a video tribute from Simon Cowell was played.

But just weeks later, while she was working in America, came the tragic news that Paul had died at the age of 55. A devastated Amanda flew back from Los Angeles and went directly to support his wife Jeanne and her daughters Lauren and Natasha at their home.

A private cremation service was followed by a public thanksgiving service at Burnham Westgate Church, attended by more than 1,200 people, including celebrities Stephen Fry and Anneka Rice. Les Dennis, whom Amanda hadn't seen or spoken to for six years, was also there with his wife, Claire. Amanda, who arrived with Chris, said she found it difficult to imagine her friend not being around.

'I can't quite accept that he's gone but the laughter, fun times and great wine we've had together over the last fifteen years will stay with me and my family for ever. I always called him the Lord Mayor of Burnham Market. He loved a bit of drama and loved being in the spotlight, and he would love it today.'

The colourful hotelier was a huge Elvis Presley fan and guests later attended a party in the gardens of the Hoste Arms, where they were entertained by an Elvis impersonator.

That October Piers Morgan confirmed rumours that he would be quitting as a judge on *Britain's Got Talent*. Veteran American chat show host Larry King was standing down from his long-running programme, *Larry King Live*, and Piers was to replace him in January, working in New York.

'I'll miss the late-night drinking sessions with Amanda, and Ant and Dec,' said Piers. 'Most of all, I'll miss winding up my co-judges and being wound up by them.'

There followed a round of fevered speculation as to who would replace him on *BGT*, with bookmakers having Louis Walsh as favourite at 2–1, followed by Sharon Osbourne at 5–2, and odds of 10–1 on Robbie Williams and *Baywatch* star David Hasselhoff. As ever, Simon milked the gossip and speculation to the limit, saying that he was in no hurry and hadn't yet made his mind up. In December 2010 the 'oracle spoke'. Simon would definitely be taking part in only the live TV shows, while David Hasselhoff and comedian Michael McIntyre would join Amanda for the auditions.

'I'm a massive fan of *Britain's Got Talent*,' said McIntyre, 'and am extremely excited to be a judge. I was so thrilled when Simon Cowell asked me that I immediately wanted to run into Ant and Dec's arms to celebrate!'

It did mean that there would be four judges at the finals stage but Simon seemed to overlook the fact that he had previously said that it didn't work with Kelly Brook.

Amanda was saddened that her 'sparring partner' Piers would no longer be there and also that Simon wouldn't be arriving until later. But she declared herself happy with the new judges. And at least Simon hadn't tried the 'glamour girl' trick again, as he had with Kelly. 'I will obviously really miss the boys because there was a brilliant chemistry but I've been a massive fan of Michael since I went to see him a few years ago. And the Hoff I just think is very funny.'

There was more exciting news for Amanda when she was asked to anchor the upcoming wedding of Prince William and Kate Middleton for CBS at Westminster Abbey on 29 April 2011. This was a prestigious job, which would enhance her position as a news broadcaster. It also reminded her of her childhood fascination with the wedding of the Prince of Wales and Lady Diana Spencer. She had kept a scrapbook of the occasion and even wrote a letter to Buckingham Palace to congratulate them.

Towards the end of the year she once more co-hosted the *Sun* Military Awards with Phillip Schofield at London's Imperial War Museum, attended by Prince Charles and Camilla along with Prime Minister David Cameron and his wife Samantha. Celebrity guests included David Beckham, Emma Bunton, Geri Halliwell, *X Factor* winner Matt Cardle, and Girls Aloud singers Kimberley Walsh and Nicola Roberts.

Among the many stories of bravery was Karl Lev, 29, who got the Most Outstanding Solider award for defusing a record 139 Taliban bombs in just 6 months. And Ricky Furgusson, 25, who risked death 4 times to help save wounded colleagues in Afghanistan before he was blown up by a hidden bomb. He lost both legs below the thigh, five fingers and an eye.

There was a heart-warming moment when Amanda asked former RAF Flight Sergeant Bill Moore, 87, to chat about old times. Then his old pal, Sergeant Peter Lovatt, 86, walked on. The pair had become great friends as they trained for war together in 1942 but had lost touch and hadn't seen each other for 68 years.

It was another night of high emotions, which rounded up yet another hectic 12 months for Amanda. A relaxing Christmas at home with the family was even more special this year because of the secret she had been harbouring.

NINETEEN

THE BIG SECRET

'No one ever guessed.'

AMANDA HOLDEN ON HER PREGNANCY

Amanda enjoyed keeping in touch with her friends and entertaining her followers with regular postings of her thoughts and activities on the Twitter social network. On Christmas Eve 2010 she had tweeted that she would be having 'nut roast' on Christmas Day and would be cooking beef for Chris because 'he's not keen on turkey'.

Following the announcement that Elton John and David Furnish had a son, Zachary, born on Christmas Day to a surrogate mother, Amanda happily tweeted, 'So thrilled for Elton John and David Furnish! How wonderful life is – when you become parents!' Two days before the New Year she said she was feeling poorly: 'Very ill in bed. Chrispy is being Florence Nightingale!' Then, to nearly everyone's great surprise, she slipped in another post at 9.55pm on 4

January 2011, which was to cause much excitement and had reporters eagerly chasing up the story.

It read, simply, 'Just to let you know. I am six months pregnant with a baby boy!! Have had to keep it quiet until now!'

As the announcement quickly spread to news outlets, and she was bombarded with good-luck messages and questions, she quickly posted a follow-up message reassuring everyone that it would not affect her work commitments: 'I'm still doing *BGT* and *Shrek the Musical*!!!'

There followed more detail on her official website. It read, 'Amanda Holden and her husband Chris Hughes are delighted to announce that Amanda is six months pregnant with their second child. Their delight is increased by the fact that last year she tragically lost a baby. As they are sure everyone will understand, they needed to get the all clear from the doctor before they shared their very happy news. Amanda, Chris and their four-year-old daughter Lexi are absolutely thrilled, and say they cannot wait to welcome the new addition to their family. Amanda will still be doing *Britain's Got Talent* Season Five and *Shrek the Musical* in London's West End.'

For once, Amanda had managed to hold on to a secret without excitedly blabbing it out. And Piers Morgan was amazed that she had kept it quiet. On his own Twitter site he commented, 'She's six months pregnant – how the hell did someone so indiscreet keep that a secret so long? Very excited for her and Chris.'

Among celebrity pals tweeting their messages of congratulations were TV presenter Holly Willoughby, who was pregnant with her second child. 'Congrats, my darling! A boy! How wonderful, bet Lexi can't wait . . . Big kiss to family Holden.' Actress Denise Van Outen wrote, 'Huge congrats to you and your family. Exciting news! Love the Meads.' And Myleene Klass – another pregnant TV presenter – added, 'HUGE congrats, gorgeous girl. Very happy for you, Chris and Lexi. More pool play dates with our babies!'

In fact, there was a swell of pregnant celebrities. Actress Sophie Dahl and her singer/pianist husband Jamie Cullum's first baby was due in February. Rod Stewart and Penny Lancaster were also expecting that month – her second child and Rod's eighth – and James Corden and his fiancée, Julia, were looking forward to being parents in March.

April babies were due for *Coronation Street* actress Kym Marsh and her *Hollyoaks* fiancé, Jamie Lomas; model Abbey Clancy and her footballer fiancé, Peter Crouch; and superstar singer Mariah Carey, who was expecting twins with her husband Nick. In January David and Victoria Beckham joined the list, when they announced that Victoria would become a mum for the fourth time in July 2011.

It was just a month after her miscarriage that Amanda was surprised to find that she was pregnant again. Just when she thought that, perhaps, she should just be happy with one child, there was expectation of a new baby once more. But, surprised and delighted as she and Chris were, they were scared that the same thing was going to happen as before. And so they were determined to keep it to themselves for as long as possible. Trying to temper her mounting excitement was difficult when she discovered it was a boy – a brother to Lexi that they had dreamed of.

In the meantime, she was concerned about her work commitments. Having gone through the stressful auditions for *Shrek* and then feeling ecstatic when she was chosen, she desperately didn't want to have to pull out. Starring in a West End stage musical was the childhood dream she had achieved when she did *Thoroughly Modern Millie* in 2003–04. It had been such an exhilarating experience that she was excitedly looking forward to being on the stage once more and could barely contemplate the thought that she wouldn't now be able to do it.

The baby was due at the end of March 2011, with the show starting two months later. She remembered how physical and exhausting the rehearsals were for *Millie* – all the dancing and singing. Could she possibly do that while pregnant? But Amanda doesn't know when to give up, it seems, and was determined that she would manage it – somehow. Nevertheless, she was apprehensive when she contacted the show's producer, Caro Newling, to tell her about the pregnancy. But, to her great relief, Newling agreed to reschedule rehearsals to fit in around her.

It had also previously been agreed that she could take a week off at the end of May and beginning of June to appear in the finals of *Britain's Got Talent*. With two 'new kids on the block' in the shape of Michael McIntyre and David Hasselhoff, Simon Cowell wanted Amanda there at all costs. She assured him that she would be able to do the auditions in January and have the baby in the gap before she would need to return for the live, televised shows a few months later.

The pregnancy craving Amanda had with Lexi – thick cheese on crusty bread – had returned and she wolfed it down with pickled onions. As Amanda's figure began to swell she managed to hide her growing tummy in public by a clever choice of clothes, body-shaping maternity lingerie, under-dresses and strategically placed handbags. And, apart from a few of her girlfriends suspecting that she had secretly had a 'boob job', she managed to conceal her secret.

'No one ever guessed. I was waiting for someone to write a piece in one of the newspapers saying I'd eaten a few too many mince pies over Christmas!' she said with a laugh.

It was hiding her morning sickness that proved to be more of a problem and, on several occasions while doing a report for *The Early Show*, she was desperately trying not to throw up.

All the time there was the worry that she might miscarry again. But after five months she began to relax a little and to be more optimistic. After almost six months of an amazing cover-up the first person Amanda told about her pregnancy was Lexi, while they were on holiday in the Maldives just before Christmas. 'Lexi put her hands on my bump and said, "Is that true life, Mama?" meaning, "Was it real?" She was asking if the baby could see her and, when we said he couldn't, she suggested feeding him carrots so he could see in the dark!'

Lexi loved the idea of having a baby brother and would often come up to Amanda, put her hands on her tummy and shout 'Helloooo!' But, despite her excitement, she was remarkably good at keeping it quiet. 'I think she quite enjoyed having a secret only the three of us shared. We went on a secret baby-clothes shop over Christmas, which Lexi loved. She even made up a story, telling the shop assistant we were buying clothes for my friend who was pregnant!'

Once it was all out in the open, Amanda felt greatly relieved. Her mum Judith was very excited and so, too, was her former nemesis turned good pal Piers Morgan, who was in line to be godfather. 'He's vying for the role and he'll probably get the job,' said Amanda with a smile. 'He's a family man – he's got three boys [from a previous marriage] and will probably have more kids with his new wife Celia. He actually seems even happier than I am about my news!'

After she had gone public with the baby news Carol Newling announced, 'The whole team on *Shrek the Musical* is thrilled for Amanda and Chris at their unexpected good news. Amanda's innate professionalism, alongside her commitment to the part of Princess Fiona, means that together, over the last few weeks, we have successfully adapted and extended the proposed rehearsal schedule around her pregnancy, allowing Amanda to fully prepare for previews at the Theatre Royal Drury Lane.'

In the enchanting story, grumpy ogre Shrek (Nigel Lindsay) and his loyal steed Donkey (Richard Blackwood) set off to confront Lord Farquaad (Nigel Harman), who has banished fairytale characters from his kingdom and exiled them to Shrek's swamp. Farquaad wants to become king but in order to do so he must marry the beautiful Princess Fiona, who is waiting for her one true love. Unfortunately, she is being guarded in a tower by a fire-breathing dragon. So he makes a deal with Shrek: rescue Fiona and bring her to him, and he will get rid of the creatures in his swamp. Shrek sets off on his mission with nervous steed Donkey. But it turns out that Fiona isn't all that she seems, for every night she turns into an ogress.

Amanda thought it a hoot the first time the green make-up, prosthetics and a wig were applied to transform her into an ogress, even though it took nearly two hours. She joked that she looked like an alien from *Doctor Who*. Lexi couldn't stop giggling when Mum showed her a picture of herself halfway through make-up in which she looked bald. And Amanda also loved waddling around in the 'fat suit' that was created for her.

By now Amanda was confident that she would be able to

juggle pregnancy, work and new baby. 'I'll be home all day when I'm doing *Shrek* and won't need to leave the house until 5 o'clock in the afternoon. I'll be doing the feeding and the cuddling during the day, and it'll be Chris who gets to do all the nasty night-times. I want to work. I've got this work ethic in me that's been instilled since childhood.'

But everything was happening at once as she embarked on rehearsals for *Shrek*, began work on auditions for *BGT* and fought against tiredness, as the baby inside her added a physical and mental strain that was growing by the day. Amanda had never shied away from a challenge. But had even *she* bitten off more than she could chew?

TWENTY

IN A FLAP

'My life is never boring!'
AMANDA HOLDEN ON HER
HECTIC SCHEDULE

Amanda was excited but apprehensive about starting work on auditions for the fifth series of *BGT* without Simon Cowell and Piers Morgan. With so much going on in her life at the moment she would have preferred the comfort of getting back and having a laugh with her old pals instead of yet more new changes. Four years of working with Simon and Piers had generated a level of bickering, banter, teasing and laughter that exists only between good friends. But they had hit it off right from the start. It had been a winning combination. What if the dynamics between Amanda, Michael McIntyre and David Hasselhoff didn't work? Worst still, suppose she didn't like them.

Chris, as ever, did his best to reassure her that all

would be well but, as the first day of auditions in London approached, she became increasingly worried and admitted that she had butterflies in her tummy that had nothing to do with the new baby's movements. But at least she would be reunited with one old face on the panel. Louis Walsh, who had stepped in for a flu-racked Simon in the last series, was back to fill in for David Hasselhoff, who was still in panto, playing Hook in *Peter Pan* at Wimbledon. He would be joining them for later auditions.

Amanda had taken Lexi to see David in panto at Christmas and she thought him excellent in the role. She later joked that he definitely wasn't one to 'buzz off'. David had been a judge alongside Piers Morgan and Sharon Osbourne on *America's Got Talent* for four years, so Simon knew what he was getting. But comedian Michael McIntyre was untried in the role.

When he was first approached by Simon, Michael joked that it felt like a *BGT* audition. 'He did all the "Cowell" things. At one point he said, "Here's one of the problems I have." I didn't know how it was going. At the end he said, "I'd really like you to be judge." I felt so honoured and excited.' He added that he thought the opportunity was too good to refuse. 'I couldn't pass it up. It's a wonderfully fun thing to do. I love watching *Britain's Got Talent* on TV – to be on it should be great fun.' The portly comic also joked that he was chosen to add some Cheryl Cole-style glamour.

Louis, who loved his stint on the show during the previous series, was thrilled at being able to return.

Outspoken as ever, he declared himself bored with dancers and acrobats because he didn't believe they could last in showbusiness. Then, in a reference that left younger fans of the show scratching their heads, he said that he wanted to discover a wacky comedian like Freddie Starr.

'I don't want to see another Diversity or Spellbound. We need more comedy, someone like Freddie Starr, who's funny but unpredictable. He was found through a talent contest and played the Royal Variety show. He always caused chaos on stage and that's what we need.'

Starr had appeared in the Royal Variety Performance in 1970 and from 1972 he was the stand out performer in the television series *Who Do You Do?*, which featured a line-up of impressionists. But none of them could match the sheer madcap antics of Freddie – most memorably his impression of Hitler in shorts and wellington boots. Freddie, 68 in January 2011, went on to have his own TV series but by the 1980s his star was fading and for the last 30 years he has seldom been seen on TV.

Louis also had an eye on other veteran acts when it came to uncovering new talent. 'I'd love it if we discovered a new Shirley Bassey, Tom Jones or Cliff Richard,' he said. 'I'm not sure what Simon Cowell would say but he won't be there this time. I'll probably cause a bit of mischief.'

On the first day of auditions Amanda made an eye-catching arrival in a pink coat but she kept her baby bulge under wraps, hidden behind a huge pink bow. Always one for putting style before comfort, she spurned maternity wear or even sensible shoes as she tottered around in towering black patent heels, clutching a pink quilted Chanel handbag. She also wore a huge smile as she waved to the hundreds of cheering fans and wannabes, and kissed and shook hands with a few well-wishers.

'I feel amazing,' she said in reply to questions about her pregnancy. 'Yes, it is a boy but we haven't picked any names yet. It's tricky.'

Michael and Louis were also cheered when they arrived and both smiled broadly before making their way inside the Hammersmith Apollo.

To her relief, Amanda soon relaxed with her fellow judges and started to have fun. During a break in auditions she wrote to her many followers on Twitter, 'It's going well! Michael is doing a grand job and Louis is ace, of course! Piers who?!!!!'

Michael felt himself turning from Mr Nice Guy into Mr Nasty as the day wore on. 'I started off being quite nice to the people who weren't very good but that's all going to change. I find the power very thrilling!' After an oddball act involving a mother and daughter who 'miaowed' an opera aria together, Michael commented, 'When it comes to the very niche area of cat singing, you were very good.'

But the judges' composure was shattered later in the day when they were 'mooned' by an unusual act in which a man peeled off several pairs of underpants! The three judges and audience watched in hysterics as the hopeful appeared on stage and started to peel off the first of five pairs of Y-fronts.

After the removal of each one he dipped them in paint and used them to create a picture until he was naked! Among other acts was a girl who read a poem with a snake around her neck and a man who squeezed into a box.

Towards the end of the day Amanda started to feel tired and kept herself going by eating lots of sweets to provide a sugar energy boost. She returned home exhausted but happy, announcing that she loved 'the new boys'. Pleased to get out of her high heels, she changed into more comfortable clothes, put her feet up and tucked into a plate of cheese and crackers.

But it was back to business the following day and she upped the glamour stakes by wearing even higher leopard-print heels, a double-breasted black coat, pink dress and dangly earrings. Her nails were painted black to match her coat and she had pulled her hair into a chic side bun.

Amanda – in motherly mode – was impressed by several child acts and Michael continued to make amusing comments that got the audience laughing but Louis was booed when he called a 19-year-old saxophone player who suffers from Asperger's syndrome 'boring'. Referring to *The X Factor*, in which Louis mentored Irish singing twins John and Edward Grimes, a.k.a. Jedward, the musician replied, 'How can you say I'm boring? You let Jedward through!' Louis shot back, 'Yeah but Jedward are making millions now!' Although the audience started to boo him, Louis refused to change his mind and the saxophonist failed to go through to the next round.

The following day Amanda's feathers were ruffled when a bird-brained comic act unnerved her with his intense eyes. His bizarre performance involved strutting up and down the stage like a pigeon, squawking, bobbing his head and flapping his arms. As the audience started to boo, all three judges buzzed him off but, still looking scary, he suddenly swooped towards them. A member of the audience who witnessed it was reported as saying, 'When the guy was on, Amanda looked freaked, and left her seat and spoke to a security guy. Then she went back to her seat, only for him to leap off the stage at the end of his performance. Amanda was straight back out of her seat and hid behind Michael McIntyre, who spun his chair round. He was hugging her while security grabbed the man.'

It later emerged that the man was Phil Zimmerman, whose pigeon act was well known on the open-mic comedy circuit. He was also a regular face on the TV music quiz *Never Mind the Buzzcocks*, in the humorous 'line-up' part of the show, in which the two teams have to guess – out of half a dozen in the line-up – who once had a hit record, either solo or with a band. Phil had rushed towards the judges simply to hand them flyers advertising his comedy club.

Amanda saw the funny side later that evening when she told Chris all about it. And the following day she laughed so much at the headline to the story in the *Sun* – SIX-FOOT PIGEON ATTACKS AMANDA – that she had it framed and put on her wall. But Phil was not so happy with the headline and any suggestion that he attacked Amanda. And he told his local newspaper, the *Ealing Gazette*, that it had been blown up out of all proportion.

After a long wait he had been the third from last act on stage, and he felt the audience and judges were getting tired and restless. 'The audience had already been sitting there for three and a half hours, and they just wanted to shout. My act is unusual and – surprise, surprise – they didn't get it. They started shouting, "Off! Off!"' By this time he had acted out two of his comedy characters: 'exploding man', which sees him go red and look as if he might pop; and 'pigeon man'. That just left him 'wolf man' but by this time Amanda had already buzzed him off. So it was in the last incarnation that he actually glared and made a gesture towards Amanda, who got up and hid by Michael's chair.

Afterwards he went to give Michael a flyer for his club but he backed off after security guards moved towards him. He said claims he was bundled off by bouncers were untrue. 'They never touched me. I saw I couldn't give the judges a flyer so I flicked one towards them and someone picked it up and gave it to them.' Phil added that his act usually went down well elsewhere but the *BGT* audience was not the usual comedy crowd he was used to. Although he acknowledged that the incident and report had considerably raised his profile, he felt that he had wanted to set the record straight. 'It's all publicity. I'm not a nutter and everyone who knows me knows that. I'm playing a character. I'm sorry if my act was a little too imaginative or subtle for the audience who were there. But I was offended by the suggestion I attacked pregnant Amanda Holden.'

With a break in the auditions until they went to Manchester the following week, where David Hasselhoff would be joining them, Amanda switched her attention to *Shrek* and began doing some dance rehearsals. She had started general dance classes back in September 2010 in order to get in shape, knowing that it would be more difficult as her pregnancy wore on. And she admitted to being nervous about the role.

'Anything you do that is live and where you put yourself up for criticism is nerve-racking. But I always say that, if I'm going to judge other people, I have to accept my own criticism. I know people think that I'm a hoofer and a singer, and I did start like that but I don't feel it's natural for me now, so I always have to work really hard.'

Now the extra weight she was carrying made it feel strange but she soon got into the swing of things and later laughed that 'tap dancing and pregnancy actually go really well together!'

One hectic morning involved her having a scan, a swine-flu jab, wig-fitting for *Shrek* and an interview with *The Times*. 'My life is never boring!' she remarked. Getting fitted for her Princess Fiona ogre head was an unusual experience. She had to stand in a bin bag while blue plastic gel then plaster of Paris was smeared across her shoulders, neck, face and head. She was unable to see anything and had two holes to breathe through, and wasn't allowed to move or talk for over an hour while it set. She later joked that remaining silent so long was 'a major challenge'.

Little Lexi loved it when Mummy took her shopping with her to buy some clothes for her new baby brother but one thing caused her some puzzlement. 'Why do the baby clothes we just bought have pockets?' she asked with a frown. 'What will he put in there?' She also made Amanda laugh when she declared, 'Mama, you're the best mummy in the whole university.' Amanda later chuckled and said, 'I think I'm raising a stand-up comedian!'

New judge David made his *BGT* debut in Manchester and proved to be as colourful a character as expected. Despite the grey skies and drizzly weather, he turned up at the city's Opera House in sunglasses and was greeted by an excited crowd who chanted 'Hoff, Hoff, Hoff'. Amanda – whose arrivals had now become her own personal fashion show – upped the glamour stakes, wearing a short white cape-style coat with her hair curled in homage to Marilyn Monroe. She was soon amused by David's home-spun maxims and baffling quasi-proverbs. His comment to one contestant, 'I may have been born yesterday but I was up all night,' had her giggling. And he would often tell nervous performers to 'breathe in God and let out a smile'. With Simon away, Amanda felt a frisson of excitement with the 'new boys'.

'It's brilliant – it's like the king's away and all his little courtiers are all playing – we've been quite naughty!' she said.

Knowing that she would be in Liverpool for Lexi's fifth birthday, Amanda and Chris arranged a party for her five days earlier. All the girls were dressed as fairies and the boys as wizards, and Lexi had so many presents that afterwards Amanda joked that her house must now contain the most pink plastic in the world.

But the whirlwind of auditions, rehearsals, make-up and costume fittings, along with pregnancy and being a wife and mother, were on Amanda's mind. One evening she had a weird dream in which she was in her cooking apron, worried about her roast potatoes burning, while on stage being a magician's assistant for *BGT*! But, despite the mental and physical exhaustion, Amanda was coping – as she said she would. Then tragedy struck.

On 1 February, the day after the final auditions in Birmingham, Amanda went to the West Middlesex Hospital in Isleworth, London, because her baby appeared to have stopped moving. She was devastated to discover that she had miscarried at seven months.

Family, friends, fans and ordinary members of the public shared her grief and messages of support flooded in. Amongst sympathisers were pregnant friends. Myleene Klass wrote, 'I'm so very sorry. Please God, watch over your family and your little angel in heaven.' And Holly Willoughby added, 'Sending you so much love x.'

Dad-to-be James Corden said, 'All my love and prayers

to Amanda Holden and Chris. X.' TV presenter Lorraine Kelly, who suffered a miscarriage herself in 2001, expressed 'sincere condolences to Amanda Holden and Chris – so sad they have lost their baby – my thoughts are with them and their families.' And Amanda's best pal, Sarah Parish, whose first child, Ella-Jayne, died due to a heart defect in 2009, wrote, 'My love and prayers go out to a very dear friend today. Keep strong my angel.'

Piers Morgan tweeted, 'So desperately sad for my special friend Amanda – sending her and Chris my love and prayers at this horrible time.' Michael McIntyre told reporters, 'Amanda is such a wonderful person. I'm heartbroken for her and Chris.' And David Hasselhoff added, 'Amanda is a first class lady. My heart goes out to her.'

Amanda shut herself away as she tried to cope with her overwhelming grief. And, once more, Chris was by her side, providing her with all the love and support she needed. But Amanda had overcome trials and tribulations in the past. She had always been a fighter and those who knew her had no doubt that, given time, she would bounce back again.

AFTERWORD

It is not unusual for little girls to dream of becoming a famous singer, actress or even a fairytale princess. And many of them go to dance or drama classes, or take music lessons. But the great majority lose the passion as they grow up and develop new interests. And they set their sights on more conventional careers or on motherhood.

A very few, like Amanda, remain focused on their childhood dream and have the determination to make it come true. Not everyone has the opportunities, of course. Amanda's extrovert mum, Judith, loved dressing up, singing, dancing and acting but was too busy bringing up Amanda and her sister Debbie to contemplate trying to make a career out of it – particularly as she was left alone to deal with them after parting from Frank.

Les Collister was to put stability as well as love and laughter back into the family, and it provided Amanda with a platform from which to launch herself to stardom. And, as always, she was brutally honest about what she wanted. Being a successful 'jobbing' actress was not good enough. She had to be famous and return home one day as a celebrity.

That little girl, who directed and starred in her own version of shows, such as *Annie* and *Grease*, in her parents' back garden, was not just playing. She had already started to learn her craft! And the other kids she cajoled into appearing in the shows were in no doubt about who was the boss.

Amanda loved going to Bishop's Waltham Little Theatre with her family and was proud of their nickname of the Von Trapps. It reinforced her belief that there was nothing more she wanted to do in life than to act. She felt comfortable on the stage, under the spotlight, where she could show off and get applause. But offstage, too, Amanda has always been an entertainer, who switches on a smile and tells a dirty joke or amusing anecdote to anyone willing to listen.

Her outspokenness and earthy – sometimes wicked – sense of humour have not always amused others. And, combined with a natural inclination to act with her heart and not her head, those qualities have often spelled trouble. She has learned some harsh lessons in life and realised how her behaviour can impact on other people.

And marriage, motherhood and maturity have diluted some of her excesses. Yet, at heart, she remains that same mischievous, enthusiastic and funny girl she has always been. She's still able to shock and embarrass others with her remarks. Often it is Chris who is left red faced. One of his nicknames for her is 'The Lip' because she has too much to say! But those who love her would have her no other way. Her sense of fun is infectious – and she has one of the dirtiest laughs around!

Amanda has never hidden her light under a bushel. Why put it there when it can be shining on her face? And she is too large a character to sit back and not be noticed. It's only at home with her family that she really switches off and becomes just mum and wife. In public she has always felt that 'the show must go on'. This colourful and gregarious personality is not to everyone's taste and it does seem that people either love her or hate her. But she is great company, kind and caring, and a loving wife and mother.

Balancing her overwhelming drive and ambition with having a family was tricky but she managed to do it. She had wanted children but knew that having them too early, when she was making her way in showbusiness, might bring about the end of her dreams. Instead, she chose the right time, with the right man – eventually.

While some may consider her ambition and 'never say no' determination to be a little too much for their liking, others see them as admirable qualities. And no one can deny her work ethic! She's worked incredibly hard to get where she is today. It hasn't fallen into her lap. She's had to get out there, face rejection and get on with it. 'Every day I'm amazed by my life. I'm here thanks to luck and hard work.'

But Amanda has never seriously wavered from her belief that she would get there in the end. Everything she has ever done – the drama classes, part-time jobs, the knocking on producers' doors – has been to progress her journey to the ultimate destination of stardom. Let us not forget that she had her Oscar winning speech written and well rehearsed at the age of nine. Later, at secondary school, she even created for herself the stage name of Beverley Saunders, which she persuaded her friends to call her.

And Amanda had an early lesson in coping with disappointment after she wrote to *Jim'll Fix It* asking the TV show's 'fixer' Jimmy Savile if he could arrange for her to dance with Legs & Co., the dancers she so loved on *Top of the Pops*. But failing even to get a reply did not put her off and she got her TV break years later on *Blind Date*.

While others would be more than happy to settle for a bit part in *EastEnders* as a stepping stone, Amanda was eagerly pushing for more and to turn market-stall holder Carmen into a major character. She didn't succeed but Amanda has always made the most of every chance she has had in life. She's never been afraid to approach producers and influential people directly, and tell them what she wants and likes and dislikes. Simon Cowell's ear, for example, has been red hot with her unashamed badgering for a children's version of *BGT* and her desire to be a judge on one of his talent shows in America.

In the end she managed to make it across the Atlantic after she and Piers Morgan were interviewed about *BGT* and the phenomenon of Susan Boyle on various US chat shows. Once again Amanda saw her opportunity and went for it, which resulted in her job on *The Early Show*.

The break Stateside came, she later said with a laugh, in the nick of time. 'I was starting to lose my dignity, dropping not-so-subtle hints to Simon about how much I wanted to work in America. So I'm really happy I didn't have to go down on my knees – unlike Piers Morgan!'

There are highs and lows in everyone's life but being in the public eye has accentuated these for Amanda Holden. She admitted her mistake in having an affair with Neil Morrissey and regretted the pain she had caused Les Dennis. An incident like this in any marriage is damaging enough but for it to be splashed all over the newspapers made it so much more difficult. Les was crushed, while Amanda was vilified as a heartless adulteress. Undoubtedly it would have been better for her public image to have appeared more remorseful, instead of partying with her girl pals but it has never been Amanda's style to wallow in misery. She copes best by confronting life with a smile and tackling adversity head on.

Her indomitable spirit has seen her bounce back time

and again – the parents who split; a broken marriage and the flak that ensued; a cancer scare; loss of her beloved grandfather Jimmy; and two miscarriages. Along the way she has received hurtful criticism for shows, such as *Mad About Alice*, *Celeb* and *Big Top*, but it is to her credit that she has never been afraid to try new things. And she has had her fair share of spectacular successes. The traditional showbiz dream of having one's name in lights became a reality with the lead role in the West End musical *Thoroughly Modern Millie* and she has starred in some of the most popular TV comedies and dramas, such as *Kiss Me Kate*, *The Grimleys*, *Cutting It* and *Wild at Heart*.

But it was the will to push herself continually – when other actors would settle for what they had – that propelled her into orbit with *Britain's Got Talent*. And it also unexpectedly opened the door to America. Now she has even fulfilled every little girl's fairytale dream by becoming a princess – in her case, in *Shrek*.

'I keep putting myself out there. I don't like playing it safe. I know exactly how the contestants feel on *Britain's Got Talent*. Like me, they're prepared to take a risk.'

Amanda did go back to sleepy Bishop's Waltham as a celebrity and opened the annual carnival that she so loved as a little girl. She has yet to read that Oscar speech for real but, given her list of remarkable achievements, who knows what lies ahead? Her drive to try new things and set new goals continues. Truly, once she sets her mind to something, there's no 'Holden' her back!

'Life is great. All my ducks are in a row,' she once said. Or, in the words of her beloved Abba, the winner takes it all.